The History of the Rise, Progress, and Accomplishment of the Abolition of the African Slave-Trade, by the British Parliament, Volume 2

The
CABINET of FREEDOM

under the supervision of

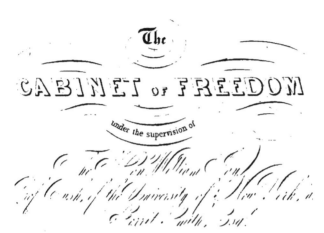

"AM I NOT A MAN AND A BROTHER"

NEW YORK.

Published by John S. Taylor

1838.

THE HISTORY

OF THE

RISE, PROGRESS, AND ACCOMPLISHMENT

OF THE

ABOLITION

OF THE

AFRICAN SLAVE-TRADE,

BY THE

BRITISH PARLIAMENT.

BY THOMAS CLARKSON, M. A,

IN THREE VOLUMES,
VOL. II.

NEW-YORK:

PUBLISHED BY JOHN S. TAYLOR,

CORNER OF PARK-ROW AND NASSAU-STREET,
OPPOSITE THE CITY HALL.

1836.

CONTENTS OF THE SECOND VOLUME.

HISTORY OF THE ABOLITION

OF THE

SLAVE-TRADE.

CHAPTER I.

AUTHOR SECURES THE GLOUCESTER PAPER, AND LAYS THE FOUNDATION
OF A PETITION FROM THAT CITY—DOES THE SAME AT WORCESTER—AND
AT CHESTER—ARRIVES AT LIVERPOOL—COLLECTS SPECIMENS OF AFRI-
CAN PRODUCE—ALSO IMPORTS AND EXPORTS—AND MUSTER-ROLLS—AND
ACCOUNTS OF DOCK-DUTIES—AND IRON INSTRUMENTS USED IN THE SLAVE-
TRADE.—HIS INTRODUCTION TO MR. NORRIS, AND OTHERS—AUTHOR AND
HIS ERRAND BECOME KNOWN—PEOPLE VISIT HIM OUT OF CURIOSITY.—
FREQUENT CONTROVERSIES ON THE SUBJECT OF THE SLAVE-TRADE.

ON my arrival at Gloucester, I waited upon
my friend Dean Tucker. He was pleased to
hear of the great progress I had made since he left
me. On communicating to him my intention
of making interest with the editors of some provincial papers, to enlighten the public mind, and
with the inhabitants of some respectable places,
for petitions to Parliament, relative to the abolition of the Slave-trade, he approved of it, and
introduced me to Mr. Raikes, the proprietor of
the respectable paper belonging to that city. Mr.
Raikes acknowledged, without any hesitation, the
pleasure he should have in serving such a noble
cause; and he promised to grant me, from time

1 *

to time, a corner in his paper, for such things
as I might point out to him for insertion. This
promise he performed afterwards, without any pecuniary consideration, and solely on the ground
of benevolence. He promised also his assistance
as to the other object, for the promotion of which
I left him several of my Summary Views to distribute.

At Worcester I trod over the same ground, and
with the same success. Timothy Bevington, of
the religious society of the Quakers, was the
only person to whom I had an introduction there.
He accompanied me to the mayor, to the editor
of the Worcester paper, and to several others,
before each of whom I pleaded the cause of the
oppressed Africans in the best manner I was able.
I dilated both on the inhumanity and on the impolicy of the trade, which I supported by the
various facts recently obtained at Bristol. I desired, however, as far as petitions were concerned,
(and this desire I expressed on all other similar occasions,) that no attempt should be made to
obtain these, till such information had been circulated on the subject, that every one, when called
upon, might judge, from his knowledge of it, how
far he would feel it right to join in it. For this
purpose I left also here several of my Summary
Views for distribution.

After my arrival at Chester, I went to the
bishop's residence, but I found he was not there.
Knowing no other person in the place, I wrote a
note to Mr. Cowdroy, whom I understood to be

the editor of the Chester paper, soliciting an interview with him. I explained my wishes to him
on both subjects. He seemed to be greatly rejoiced, when we met, that such a measure as that
of the abolition of the Slave-trade was in contemplation. Living at so short a distance from Liverpool, and in a county from which so many persons were constantly going to Africa, he was by
no means ignorant, as some were, of the nature of
this cruel traffic ; but yet he had no notion that I
had probed it so deeply, or that I had brought to
light such important circumstances concerning it,
as he found by my conversation. He made me a
hearty offer of his services on this occasion, and
this expressly without fee or reward. I accepted
them most joyfully and gratefully. It was, indeed,
a most important thing, to have a station so near
the enemy's camp, where we could watch their
motions, and meet any attack which might be
made from it. And this office of a sentinel Mr.
Cowdroy performed with great vigilance ; and
when he afterwards left Chester for Manchester,
to establish a paper there, he carried with him the
same friendly disposition towards our cause.

My first introduction at Liverpool was to William Rathbone, a member of the religious society
of the Quakers. He was the same person, who
before the formation of our committee, had procured me copies of several of the muster-rolls of
the slave-vessels belonging to that port, so that,
though we were not personally known, yet we
were not strangers to each other. Isaac Hadwen,

a respectable member of the same society, was the
person whom I saw next. I had been introduced
to him, previously to my journey, when he was
at London, at the yearly meeting of the Quakers,
so that no letter to him was necessary. As Mr.
Roscoe had generously given the profits of The
Wrongs of Africa to our committee, I made no
scruple of calling upon him. His reception of me
was very friendly, and he introduced me afterwards to Dr. Currie, who had written the preface
to that poem. There was also a fourth, upon
whom I called, though I did not know him. His
name was Edward Rushton. He had been an
officer in a slave-ship, but had lost his sight, and
had become an enemy to that trade. On passing
through Chester, I had heard, for the first time,
that he had published a poem called West-Indian
Eclogues, with a view of making the public better
acquainted with the evil of the Slave-trade, and
of exciting their indignation against it. Of the
three last it may be observed, that, having come
forward thus early, as laborers, they deserve to be
put down, as I have placed them in the map,
among the forerunners and coadjutors in this
great cause, for each published his work before
any efforts were made publicly, or without knowing that any were intended. Rushton, also, had
the boldness, though then living in Liverpool, to
affix his name to his work. These were the only
persons whom I knew for some time after my
arrival in that place.

It may not, perhaps, be necessary to enter so

largely into my proceedings at Liverpool as at Bristol. The following account, therefore, may suffice.

In my attempts to add to my collection of speci- _I_: ſol.
mens of African produce, I was favored with a sample of gum ruber astringens, of cotton from the Gambia, of indigo and musk, of long pepper, of black pepper from Whidah, of mahogany from Calabar, and of clothes of different colors, made by the natives, which, while they gave other proofs of the quality of their own cotton, gave proofs, also, of the variety of their dyes.

I made interest at the Custom-house for various exports and imports, and for copies of the muster-rolls of several slave-vessels, besides those of vessels employed in other trades.

By looking out constantly for information on this great subject, I was led to the examination of a printed card or table of the dock-duties of Liverpool, which was published annually. The town of Liverpool had so risen in opulence and importance, from only a fishing-village, that the corporation seemed to have a pride in giving a public view of this increase. Hence they published and circulated this card. Now the card contained one, among other facts, which was almost as precious, in a political point of view, as any I had yet obtained. It stated, that in the year 1772, when I knew that a hundred vessels sailed out of Liverpool for the coast of Africa, the dock-duties amounted to 4552l. and that in 1779, when I knew that, in consequence of the war, only eleven went from thence to the same coast, they amounted to 4957l. From these facts, put together, two conclusions were obvious. The first was, that the opulence of Liverpool, as far as the entry of vessels into its ports, and the dock-duties arising from thence, were concerned, was not indebted to the Slave-trade; for these duties were highest when it had only eleven ships in that employ. The second was, that there had been almost a practical experiment with respect to the abolition of it; for the vessels in it had been gradually reduced from one hundred to eleven, and yet the West Indians had not complained of their ruin, nor had the merchants or manufacturers suffered, nor had Liverpool been affected by the change.

There were specimens of articles in Liverpool, which I entirely overlooked at Bristol, and which I believe I should have overlooked here, also, had it not been for seeing them at a window in a shop; I mean those of different iron instruments used in this cruel traffic. I bought a pair of the iron hand-cuffs with which the men slaves are confined. The right hand wrist of one, and the left of another, are almost brought into contact by these, and fastened together, as the figure A in the annexed plate represents, by a little bolt with a small padlock at the end of it. I bought also a pair of shackles for the legs. These are represented by the figure B. The right ancle of one man is fastened to the left of another, as the reader will observe, by similar means. I bought

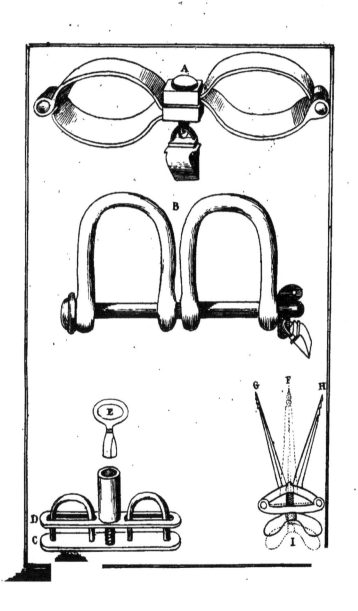

these, not because it was difficult to conceive how the unhappy victims of this execrable trade were confined, but to show the fact that they were so. For what was the inference from it, but that they did not leave their own country willingly; that, when they were in the holds of the slave-vessels, they were not in the Elysium which had been represented; and that there was a fear, either that they would make their escape, or punish their oppressors? I bought also a thumb-screw at this shop. The thumbs are put into this instrument through the two circular holes at the top of it. By turning a key, a bar rises up by means of a screw from C to D, and the pressure upon them becomes painful. By turning it further you may make the blood start from the ends of them. By taking the key away, as at E, you leave the tortured person in agony, without any means of extricating himself or of being extricated by others. This screw, as I was then informed, was applied by way of punishment, in case of obstinacy in the slaves, or for any other reputed offence, at the discretion of the captain. At the same place I bought another instrument which I saw. It was called a speculum oris. The dotted lines in the figure on the right hand of the screw, represent it when shut, the black lines when open. It is opened, as at G H, by a screw below with a knob at the end of it. This instrument is known among surgeons, having been invented to assist them in wrenching open the mouth as in the case of a locked jaw. But

it had got into use in this trade. On asking the
seller of the instruments, on what occasion it was
used there, he replied, that the slaves were frequently so sulky as to shut their mouths against
all sustenance, and this with a determination to
die ; and that it was necessary their mouth should
be forced open to throw in nutriment, that they
who had purchased them might incur no loss by
their death.

The town's talk of Liverpool was much of the
same nature as that at Bristol on the subject of
this trade. Horrible facts concerning it were
in every body's mouth. But they were more
numerous, as was likely to be the case, where
eighty vessels were employed from one port, and
only eighteen from the other. The people too at
Liverpool seemed to be more hardened, or they
related them with more coldness or less feeling.
This may be accounted for, from the greater
number of those facts, as just related, the mention of which, as it was of course more frequent,
occasioned them to lose their power of exciting
surprise. All this I thought in my favor, as I
should more easily, or with less obnoxiousness,
come to the knowledge of what I wanted to
obtain.

My friend William Rathbone, who had been
looking out to supply me with intelligence, but
who was desirous that I should not be imposed
upon, and that I should get it from the fountain-
head, introduced me to Mr. Norris for this purpose. Norris had been formerly a slave-captain,

but had quitted the trade and settled as a merchant in a different line of business. He was a man of quick penetration, and of good talents, which he had cultivated to advantage, and he had a pleasing address both as to speech and manners. He received me with great politeness, and offered me all the information I desired. I was with him five or six times at his own house for this purpose. The substance of his communications on these occasions I shall now put down, and I beg the reader's particular attention to it, as he will be referred to it in other parts of this work.

With respect to the produce of Africa, Mr. Norris enumerated many articles in which a new and valuable trade might be opened, of which he gave me one, namely, the black pepper from Whidah before mentioned. This he gave me, to use his own expressions, as one argument among many others of the impolicy of the Slave-trade, which, by turning the attention of the inhabitants to the persons of one another for sale, hindered foreigners from discovering, and themselves from cultivating, many of the valuable productions of their own soil.

On the subject of procuring slaves he gave it as his decided opinion, that many of the inhabitants of Africa were kidnapped by each other, as they were travelling on the roads, or fishing in the creeks, or cultivating their little spots. Having learnt their language, he had collected the fact from various quarters, but more particularly from the accounts of slaves, whom he had transported

in his own vessels. With respect however to
Whidah, many came from thence, who were reduced to slavery in a different manner. The king
of Dahomey, whose life (with the wars and customs of the Dahomans) he said he was then writing, and who was a very despotic prince, made no
scruple of seizing his own subjects, and of selling
them, if he was in want of any of the articles
which the slave-vessels would afford him. The
history of this prince's life he lent me afterwards
to read, while it was yet in manuscript, in which
I observed that he had recorded all the facts now
mentioned. Indeed he made no hesitation to state
them, either when we were by ourselves, or when
others were in company with us. He repeated
them at one time in the presence both of Mr.
Cruden, and of Coupland. The latter was then
a slave-merchant at Liverpool. He seemed to be
fired at the relation of these circumstances. Unable to restrain himself longer, he entered into a
defence of the trade, both as to the humanity and
the policy of it. But Mr. Norris took up his arguments in both these cases, and answered them in
a solid manner.

With respect to the Slave-trade, as it affected
the health of our seamen, Mr. Norris admitted it
to be destructive. But I did not stand in need of
this information, as I knew this part of the subject, in consequence of my familiarity with the
muster-rolls, better than himself.

He admitted it also to be true, that they were
too frequently ill-treated in this trade. A day

or two after our conversation on this latter subject he brought me the manuscript journal of a
voyage to Africa, which had been kept by a mate,
with whom he was then acquainted. He brought
it to me to read, as it might throw some light
upon the subject on which we had talked last. In
this manuscript various instances of cruel usage
towards seamen were put down, from which it
appeared that the mate, who wrote it, had not
escaped himself.

At the last interview we had, he seemed to be
so satisfied of the inhumanity, injustice, and impolicy of the trade, that he made me a voluntary
offer of certain clauses, which he had been thinking of, and which, he believed, if put into an act of
Parliament, would judiciously effect its abolition.
The offer of these clauses I embraced eagerly.
He dictated them, and I wrote. I wrote them in
a small book which I had then in my pocket.
They were these :—

No vessel under a heavy penalty to supply
foreigners with slaves.

Every vessel to pay to government a tax for a
register on clearing out to supply our own islands
with slaves.

Every such vessel to be prohibited from purchasing or bringing home any of the productions
of Africa.

Every such vessel to be prohibited from bringing home a passenger, or any article of produce,
from the West Indies.

A bounty to be given to every vessel trading in

the natural productions of Africa. This bounty
to be paid in part out of the tax arising from the
registers of the slave-vessels.

Certain establishments to be made by government in Africa, in the Bananas, in the Isles de
Los, on the banks of the Camaranca, and in other
places, for the encouragement and support of the
new trade to be substituted there.

Such then were the services, which Mr. Norris,
at the request of William Rathbone, rendered me
at Liverpool, during my stay there; and I have
been very particular in detailing them, because I
shall be obliged to allude to them, as I have before
observed, on some important occasions in a future
part of the work.

On going my rounds one day, I met accidentally with captain Chaffers. This gentleman
either was or had been in the West India employ.
His heart had beaten in sympathy with mine, and
he had greatly favored our cause. He had seen
me at Mr. Norris's, and learned my errand there.
He told me he could introduce me in a few minutes, as we were then near at hand, to captain
Lace, if I chose it. Captain Lace, he said, had
been long in the Slave-trade, and could give me
very accurate information about it. I accepted his
offer. On talking to captain Lace, relative to the
productions of Africa, he told me that mahogany
grew at Calabar. He began to describe a tree of
that kind, which he had seen there. This tree
was from about eighteen inches to two feet in
diameter, and about sixty feet high, or, as he

expressed it, of the height of a tall chimney. As soon as he mentioned Calabar, a kind of horror came over me. His name became directly associated in my mind with the place. It almost instantly occurred to me, that he commanded the Edgar out of Liverpool, when the dreadful massacre there, as has been related, took place. Indeed I seemed to be so confident of it, that, attending more to my feelings than to my reason at this moment, I accused him with being concerned in it. This produced great confusion among us. For he looked incensed at captain Chaffers, as if he had introduced me to him for this purpose. Captain Chaffers again seemed to be all astonishment that I should have known of this circumstance, and to be vexed that I should have mentioned it in such a manner. I was also in a state of trembling myself. Captain Lace could only say it was a bad business. But he never defended himself, nor those concerned in it. And we soon parted, to the great joy of us all.

Soon after this interview I began to perceive that I was known in Liverpool, as well as the object for which I came. Mr. Coupland, the slave-merchant, with whom I had disputed at Mr. Norris's house, had given the alarm to those who were concerned in the trade, and captain Lace, as may be now easily imagined, had spread it. This knowledge of me and of my errand was almost immediately productive of two effects, the first of which I shall now mention.

I had a private room at the King's Arms tavern,

2 *

besides my bedroom, where I used to meditate
and to write. But I generally dined in public.
The company at dinner had hitherto varied but
little as to number, and consisted of those, both
from the town and country, who had been accustomed to keep up a connexion with the house.
But now things were altered, and many people
came to dine there daily with a view of seeing me,
as if I had been some curious creature imported
from foreign parts. They thought, also, they
could thus have an opportunity of conversing with
me. Slave-merchants and slave-captains came in
among others for this purpose. I had observed
this difference in the number of our company for
two or three days. Dale, the master of the tavern,
had observed it also, and told me in a good
natured manner, that many of these were my
visiters, and that I was likely to bring him a great
deal of custom. In a little time, however, things
became serious ; for they, who came to see me,
always started the abolition of the Slave-trade as
the subject for conversation. Many entered into
the justification of this trade with great warmth,
as if to ruffle my temper, or at any rate to provoke
me to talk. Others threw out, with the same
view, that men were going about to abolish it,
who would have done much better if they had
staid at home. Others said they had heard
of a person turned mad, who had conceived the
thought of destroying Liverpool, and all its glory.
Some gave as a toast, Success to the Trade, and
then laughed immoderately, and watched me

when I took my glass to see if I would drink it.
I saw the way in which things were now going,
and I believed it would be proper that I should
come to some fixed resolutions ; such as, whether
I should change my lodgings, and whether I
should dine in private ; and if not, what line of
conduct it would become me to pursue on such
occasions. With respect to changing my lodgings
and dining in private, I conceived, if I were to
do either of these things, that I should be showing an unmanly fear of my visiters, which they
would turn to their own advantage.   I conceived
too, that, if I chose to go on as before, and enter
into conversation with them on the subject of the
abolition of the Slave-trade, I might be able, by
having such an assemblage of persons daily, to
gather all the arguments which they could collect
on the other side of our question, an advantage
which I should one day feel in the future management of the cause. With respect to the line,
which I should pursue in the case of remaining
in the place of my abode and in my former habits,
I determined never to start the subject of the abolition myself ; never to abandon it when started ;
never to defend it but in a serious and dignified
manner ; and never to discover any signs of irrita-
tion, whatever provocation might be given me.
By this determination I abided rigidly.   The
King's Arms became now daily the place for discussion on this subject.   Many tried to insult me,
but to no purpose.   In all these discussions I
found the great advantage of having brought Mr.

Falconbridge with me from Bristol; for he was always at the table; and when my opponents, with a disdainful look, tried to ridicule my knowledge, among those present, by asking me if I had ever been on the coast of Africa myself, he used generally to reply, "But I have. I know all your proceedings there, and that his statements are true." These and other words put in by him, who was an athletic and resolute-looking man, were of great service to me. All disinterested persons, of whom there were four or five daily in the room, were uniformly convinced by our arguments, and took our part, and some of them very warmly. Day after day we beat our opponents out of the field, as many of the company acknowledged, to their no small mortification, in their presence. Thus, while we served the cause by discovering all that could be said against it, we served it by giving numerous individuals proper ideas concerning it, and of interesting them in our favor.

The second effect which I experienced was, that from this time I could never get any one to come forward as an evidence to serve the cause. There were, I believe, hundreds of persons in Liverpool, and in the neighborhood of it, who had been concerned in this traffic, and who had left it, all of whom could have given such testimony concerning it as would have insured its abolition. But none of them would now speak out. Of these indeed there were some, who were alive to the horrors of it, and who lamented that it should still continue. But yet even these were backward in supporting me. All that they did was just privately to see me, to tell me that I was right, and to exhort me to persevere : but as to coming forward to be examined publicly, my object was so unpopular, and would become so much more so when brought into parliament, that they would have their houses pulled down, if they should then appear as public instruments in the annihilation of the trade. With this account I was obliged to rest satisfied ; nor could I deny, when I considered the spirit, which had manifested itself, and the extraordinary number of interested persons in the place, that they had some reason for their fears; and that these fears were not groundless, appeared afterwards ; for Dr. Binns, a respectable physician belonging to the religious society of the Quakers, and to whom Isaac Hadwen had introduced me, was near falling into a mischievous plot, which had been laid against him, because he was one of the subscribers to the Institution for the Abolition of the Slave-trade, and because he was suspected of having aided me in promoting that object.

CHAPTER II.

HOSTILE DISPOSITION TOWARDS THE AUTHOR INCREASES, ON ACCOUNT OF HIS KNOWN PATRONAGE OF THE SEAMEN EMPLOYED IN THE SLAVE-TRADE.—MANNER OF PROCURING AND PAYING THEM AT LIVERPOOL—THEIR TREATMENT AND MORTALITY.—ACCOUNT OF THE MURDER OF PETER GREEN—TROUBLE TAKEN BY THE AUTHOR TO TRACE IT—HIS NARROW ESCAPE—GOES TO LANCASTER—BUT RETURNS TO LIVERPOOL—LEAVES THE LATTER PLACE.

IT has appeared that a number of persons used to come and see me, out of curiosity, at the King's Arms tavern ; and that these manifested a bad disposition towards me, which was near breaking out into open insult. Now the cause of all this was, as I have observed, the knowledge which people had obtained, relative to my errand at this place. But this hostile disposition was increased by another circumstance, which I am now to mention. I had been so shocked at the treatment of the seamen belonging to the slave-vessels at Bristol, that I determined, on my arrival at Liverpool, to institute an inquiry concerning it there also. I had made considerable progress in it, so that few seamen were landed from such vessels, but I had some communication with them ; and though no one else would come near me, to give me any information about the trade, these were always forward to speak to me, and to tell me their grievances, if it were only with the hope of being able to get redress. The consequence of this was, that they used to come to the King's Arms tavern to

see me.   Hence one, two, and three were almost
daily to be found about the door; and this happened quite as frequently after the hostility just
mentioned had shown ·itself, as before.   They,
therefore, who came to visit me out of curiosity,
could not help seeing my sailor visiters; and on
inquiring into their errand, they became more
than ever incensed against me.

The first result of this increased hostility towards me was an application from some of them
to the master of the tavern, that he would not
harbor me.   This he communicated to me in a
friendly manner, but he was by no means desirous
that I should leave him.   On the other hand, he
hoped I would stay long enough to accomplish my
object.   I thought it right, however, to take the
matter into consideration; and, having canvassed
it, I resolved to remain with him, for the reasons
mentioned in the former chapter.   But, that I
might avoid doing any thing that would be injurious to his interest, as well as in some measure
avoid giving unnecessary offence to others, I took
lodgings in Williamson Square, where I retired
to write, and occasionally to sleep, and to which
place all seamen, desirous of seeing me, were
referred.   Hence I continued to get the same information as before, but in a less obnoxious and
injurious manner.

The history of the seamen employed in the
slave-vessels belonging to the port of Liverpool,
I found to be similar to that of those from Bristol.

They, who went into this trade, were of two

classes. The first consisted of those who were ignorant of it, and to whom, generally, improper representations of advantage had been made, for the purpose of enticing them into it. The second consisted of those, who, by means of a regular system, kept up by the mates and captains, had been purposely brought by their landlords into distress, from which they could only be extricated by going into this hateful employ. How many have I seen, with tears in their eyes, put into boats, and conveyed to vessels, which were then lying at the Black Rock, and which were only waiting to receive them to sail away!

The manner of paying them in the currency of the islands was the same as at Bristol. But this practice was not concealed at Liverpool, as it was at the former place. The articles of agreement were printed, so that all, who chose to buy, might read them. At the same time it must be observed, that seamen were never paid in this manner in any other employ; and that the African wages, though nominally higher for the sake of procuring hands, were thus made to be actually lower than in other trades.

The loss by death was so similar, that it did not signify whether the calculation on a given number was made either at this or the other port. I had, however, a better opportunity at this, than I had at the other, of knowing the loss as it related to those, whose constitutions had been ruined, or who had been rendered incapable, by disease, of continuing their occupation at sea. For the slave-vessels, which returned to Liverpool, sailed immediately into the docks, so that I saw at once their sickly and ulcerated crews. The number of vessels, too, was so much greater from this, than from any other port, that their sick made a more conspicuous figure in the infirmary. And they were seen also more frequently in the streets.

With respect to their treatment, nothing could be worse. It seemed to me to be but one barbarous system from the beginning to the end. I do not say barbarous, as if premeditated, but it became so in consequence of the savage habits gradually formed by a familiarity with miserable sights, and with a course of action inseparable from the trade. Men in their first voyages usually disliked the traffic; and, if they were happy enough then to abandon it, they usually escaped the disease of a hardened heart. But if they went a second and a third time, their disposition became gradually changed. It was impossible for them to be accustomed to carry away men and women by force, to keep them in chains, to see their tears, to hear their mournful lamentations, to behold the dead and the dying, to be obliged to keep up a system of severity amidst all this affliction; in short, it was impossible for them to be witnesses, and this for successive voyages, to the complicated mass of misery passing in a slave-ship, without losing their finer feelings, or without contracting those habits of moroseness and cruelty, which would brutalize their

nature. Now, if we consider that persons could
not easily become captains (and to these the barbarities were generally chargeable by actual per-
petration, or by consent) till they had been two
or three voyages in this employ, we shall see the
reason why it would be almost a miracle, if they
who were thus employed in it, were not rather to
become monsters, than to continue to be men.

While I was at Bristol, I heard from an officer
of the Alfred, who gave me the intelligence privately, that the steward of a Liverpool ship, whose
name was Green, had been murdered in that
ship. The Alfred was in Bonny river at the same
time, and his own captain (so infamous for his
cruelty, as has been before shown) was on board
when it happened. The circumstances, he said,
belonging to this murder, were, if report were
true, of a most atrocious nature, and deserved
to be made the subject of inquiry. As to the
murder itself, he observed, it had passed as a
notorious and uncontradicted fact.

This account was given me just as I had made
an acquaintance with Mr. Falconbridge, and I
informed him of it. He said he had no doubt of
its truth. For in his last voyage he went to Bonny himself, where the ship was then lying, in
which the transaction happened. The king and
several of the black traders told him of it. The
report then current was simply this, that the steward had been barbarously beaten one evening;
that after this he was let down with chains
upon him into a boat, which was alongside of

the ship, and that the next morning he was found dead.

On my arrival at Liverpool, I resolved to inquire into the truth of this report. On looking into one of the wet docks, I saw the name of the vessel alluded to. I walked over the decks of several others, and got on board her. Two people were walking up and down her, and one was leaning upon a rail by the side. I asked the latter how many slaves this ship had carried in her last voyage. He replied, he could not tell; but one of the two persons walking about could answer me, as he had sailed out and returned in her. This man came up to us, and joined in conversation. He answered my question and many others, and would have shown me the ship. But on asking him how many seamen had died on the voyage, he changed his manner, and said, with apparent hesitation, he could not tell. I asked him next, what had become of the steward Green. He said, he believed he was dead. I asked how the seamen had been used. He said, not worse than others. I then asked whether Green had been used worse than others. He replied, he did not then recollect. I found that he was now quite upon his guard, and as I could get no satisfactory answer from him I left the ship.

On the next day, I looked over the muster-roll of this vessel. On examining it, I found that sixteen of the crew had died. I found also the name of Peter Green. I found, again, that the latter had been put down among the dead. I ob-

served also, that the ship had left Liverpool on the
fifth of June 1786, and had returned on the fifth
of June 1787, and that Peter Green was put down
as having died on the nineteenth of September;
from all which circumstances it was evident that
he must, as my Bristol information asserted, have
died upon the Coast.

Notwithstanding this extraordinary coincidence
of name, mortality, time, and place, I could gain
no further intelligence about the affair till within
about ten days before I left Liverpool; when
among the seamen, who came to apply to me in
Williamson Square, was George Ormond. He
came to inform me of his own ill usage; from
which circumstance I found that he had sailed
in the same ship with Peter Green. This led me
to inquire into the transaction in question, and I
received from him the following account:

Peter Green had been shipped as steward. A
black woman, of the name of Rodney, went out in
the same vessel. She belonged to the owners of
it, and was to be an interpretess to the slaves who
should be purchased. About five in the evening,
some time in the month of September, the vessel
then lying in Bonny river, the captain, as was his
custom, went on shore. In his absence, Rodney,
the black woman, asked Green for the keys of
the pantry; which he refused her, alleging that
the captain had already beaten him for having
given them to her on a former occasion, when she
drank the wine. The woman being passionate,

struck him, and a scuffle ensued, out of which Green extricated himself as well as he could.

When the scuffle was over the woman retired to the cabin, and appeared pensive.   Between eight and nine in the evening, the captain, who was attended by the captain of the Alfred, came on board.   Rodney immediately ran to him, and informed him that Green had made an assault upon her.   The captain, without any inquiry, beat him severely, and ordered his hands to be made fast to some bolts on the starboard side of the ship and under the half deck, and then flogged him himself, using the lashes of the cat-of-nine-tails upon his back at one time, and the double-walled knot at the end of it upon his head at another ; and stopping to rest at intervals, and using each hand alternately, that he might strike with the greater severity.

The pain had now become so very severe, that Green cried out, and entreated the captain of the Alfred, who was standing by, to pity his hard case, and to intercede for him.   But the latter replied, that he would have served him in the same manner.   · Unable to find a friend here, he called upon the chief mate ; but this only made matters worse, for the captain then ordered the latter to flog him also ; which he did for some time, using however only the lashes of the instrument.   Green then called in his distress upon the second mate to speak for him ; but the second mate was immediately ordered to perform the same cruel office, and was made to persevere in

it till the lashes were all worn into threads. But
the barbarity did not close here; for the captain,
on seeing the instrument now become useless,
ordered another, with which he flogged him as
before, beating him at times over the head with
the double-walled knot, and changing his hands,
and cursing his own left hand for not being able
to strike so severe a blow as his right.

The punishment, as inflicted by all parties, had
now lasted two hours and a half, when George
Ormond was ordered to cut down one of the arms,
and the boatswain the other, from the places of
their confinement. This being done, Green lay
motionless on the deck. He attempted to utter
something. Ormond understood it to be the word
water. But no water was allowed him. The
captain, on the other hand, said he had not yet
done with him, and ordered him to be confined
with his arms across, his right hand to his left foot,
and his left hand to his right foot. For this purpose the carpenter brought shackles, and George
Ormond was compelled to put them on. The
captain then ordered some tackle to be made fast
to the limbs of the said Peter Green, in which
situation he was then hoisted up, and afterwards
let down into a boat, which was lying alongside
the ship. Michael Cunningham was then sent to
loose the tackle, and to leave him there.

In the middle watch, or between one and two
next morning, George Ormond looked out of one
of the port-holes, and called to Green, but received
no answer. Between two and three, Paul Berry,

a seaman, was sent down into the boat and found him dead. He made his report to one of the officers of the ship. About five in the morning, the body was brought up, and laid on the waist near the half-deck door. The captain on seeing the body, when he rose, expressed no concern, but ordered it to be knocked out of irons, and to be buried at the usual place of interment for seamen, on Bonny Point. I may now observe, that the deceased was in good health before the punishment took place, and in high spirits; for he played upon the flute only a short time before Rodney asked him for the keys, while those seamen, who were in health, danced.

On hearing this cruel relation from George Ormond, who was throughout a material witness to the scene, I had no doubt in my own mind of the truth of it. But I thought it right to tell him at once that I had seen a person, about four weeks ago, who had been the same voyage with him and Peter Green, but yet who had no recollection of these circumstances. Upon this he looked quite astonished, and began to grow angry. He maintained he had seen the whole. He had also held the candle himself during the whole punishment. He asserted that one candle and half of another were burnt out while it lasted. He said also that, while the body lay in the waist, he had handled the abused parts, and had put three of his fingers into a hole, made by the double-walled knot, in the head, from whence a quantity of blood, and, he believed, brains issued. He then challenged me to bring the man before him. I desired him upon this to be cool, and to come to me the next day, and I would then talk with him again upon the subject.

In the interim I consulted the muster-roll of the vessel again. I found the name of George Ormond. He had sailed in her out of Liverpool, and had been discharged at the latter end of January in the West Indies, as he had told me. I found also the names of Michael Cunningham and of Paul Berry, whom he had mentioned. It was obvious also that Ormond's account of the captain of the Alfred being on board at the time of the punishment, tallied with that given me at Bristol by an officer of that vessel, and that his account of letting down Peter Green into the boat tallied with that, which Mr. Falconbridge, as I mentioned before, had heard from the king and the black traders in Bonny river.

When he came to me next day, he came in high spirits. He said he had found out the man whom I had seen. The man, however, when he talked to him about the murder of Peter Green, acknowledged every thing concerning it. Ormond intimated that this man was to sail again in the same ship under the promise of being an officer, and that he had been kept on board, and had been enticed to a second voyage, for no other purpose than that he might be prevented from divulging. the matter. I then asked Ormond, whether he .thought the man would acknowledge the murder in my hearing. He replied, that if I were present, he thought he would not say much about it, as he was soon to be under the same captain, but that he would not deny it. If however I were out of sight, though I might be in hearing, he believed he would acknowledge the facts.

By the assistance of Mr. Falconbridge, I found a public house, which had two rooms in it. Nearly at the top of the partition between them was a small window, which a person might look through by standing upon a chair. I desired Ormond, one evening to invite the man into the larger room, in which he was to have a candle, and to talk with him on the subject. I purposed to station myself in the smallest in the dark, so that by looking through the window I could both see and hear him, and yet be unperceived myself. The room, in which I was to be, was one, where the dead were frequently carried to be owned. We were all in our places at the time appointed. I directly discovered that it was the same man with whom I had conversed on board the ship in the wet docks.

I heard him distinctly relate many of the particulars of the murder, and acknowledge them all. Ormond, after having talked with him some time, said, "Well, then, you believe Peter Green was actually murdered?" He replied, "If Peter Green was not murdered, no man ever was." What followed I do not know. I had heard quite enough; and the room was so disagreeable in smell, that I did not choose to stay in it longer than was absolutely necessary.

I own I was now quite satisfied that the murder had taken place, and my first thought was to
bring the matter before the mayor, and to take up
three of the officers of the ship. But, in mentioning my intention to my friends, I was dissuaded
from it. They had no doubt but that in Liverpool, as there was now a notion that the Slave-
trade would become a subject of parliamentary
inquiry, every effort would be made to overthrow
me. They were of opinion also that such of the
magistrates, as were interested in the trade, when
applied to for warrants of apprehension, would
contrive to give notice to the officers to escape.
In addition to this they believed, that so many in
the town were already incensed against me, that
I should be torn to pieces, and the house where
I lodged burnt down, if I were to make the attempt. I thought it right therefore to do nothing
for the present; but I sent Ormond to London,
to keep him out of the way of corruption, till I
should make up my mind as to further proceedings on the subject.

It is impossible, if I observe the bounds I have
prescribed myself, and I believe the reader will
be glad of it on account of his own feelings, that
I should lay open the numerous cases, which
came before me at Liverpool, relative to the ill
treatment of the seamen in this wicked trade. It
may be sufficient to say, that they harrassed my
constitution, and affected my spirits daily. They
were in my thoughts on my pillow after I retired
to rest, and I found them before my eyes when I

awoke. Afflicting, however, as they were, they were of great use in the promotion of our cause. For they served, whatever else failed, as a stimulus to perpetual energy. They made me think light of former labors, and they urged me imperiously to new. And here I may observe, that among the many circumstances, which ought to excite our joy on considering the great event of the abolition of the Slave-trade, which has now happily taken place, there are few for which we ought to be more grateful, than that from this time our commerce ceases to breed such abandoned wretches ; while those, who have thus been bred in it, and who may yet find employment in other trades, will in the common course of nature be taken off in a given time, so that our marine will at length be purified from a race of monsters, which have helped to cripple its strength, and to disgrace its character.

The temper of many of the interested people of Liverpool had now become still more irritable, and their hostility more apparent than before. I received anonymous letters, entreating me to leave it, or I should otherwise never leave it alive. The only effect, which this advice had upon me, was to make me more vigilant when I went out at night. I never stirred out at this time without Mr. Falconbridge. And he never accompanied me without being well armed. Of this, however, I knew nothing until we had left the place. There was certainly a time, when I had reason to believe that I had a narrow escape. I was one day on the pier-head with many others looking at some little boats below at the time of a heavy gale. Several persons, probably out of curiosity, were hastening thither. I had seen all I intended to see, and was departing, when I noticed eight or nine persons making towards me. I was then only about eight or nine yards from the precipice of the pier, but going from it. I expected that they would have divided to let me through them; instead of which they closed upon me, and bore me back. I was borne within a yard of the precipice, when I discovered my danger; and perceiving among them the murderer of Peter Green, and two others who had insulted me at the King's Arms, it instantly struck me that they had a design to throw me over the pier-head; which they might have done at this time, and yet have pleaded that I had been killed by accident. There was not a moment to lose. Vigorous on account of the danger, I darted forward. One of them, against whom I pushed myself, fell down. Their ranks were broken. And I escaped, not without blows, amidst their imprecations and abuse.

I determined now to go to Lancaster, to make some inquiries about the Slave-trade there. I had a letter of introduction to William Jepson, one of the religious society of the Quakers, for this purpose. I found from him, that, though there were slave-merchants at Lancaster, they made their outfits at Liverpool, as a more convenient port. I learnt too from others, that the captain of the last vessel, which had sailed out of

Lancaster to the coast of Africa for slaves, had taken off so many of the natives treacherously, that any other vessel known to come from it would be cut off. There were only now one or two super-annuated captains living in the place. Finding I could get no oral testimony, I was introduced into the custom-house. Here I just looked over the muster-rolls of such slave-vessels as had formerly sailed from this port; and having found that the loss of seamen was precisely in the same proportion as elsewhere, I gave myself no further trouble, but left the place.

On my return to Liverpool, I was informed by Mr. Falconbridge, that a ship-mate of Ormond, of the name of Patrick Murray, who had been discharged in the West Indies, had arrived there. This man, he said, had been to call upon me in my absence, to seek redress for his own bad usage; but in the course of conversation he had confirmed all the particulars as stated by Ormond, relative to the murder of Peter Green. On consulting the muster-roll of the ship, I found his name, and that he had been discharged in the West Indies on the second of February. I determined therefore to see him. I cross-examined him in the best manner I could. I could neither make him contradict himself, nor say any thing that militated against the testimony of Ormond. I was convinced therefore of the truth of the transaction; and, having obtained his consent, I sent him to London to stay with the latter, till he should hear further from me. I learnt also from Mr. Falconbridge, that my

visiters had continued to come to the King's Arms
during my absence ; that they had been very liberal of their abuse of me ; and that one of them
did not hesitate to say (which is remarkable) that
" I deserved to be thrown over the pier-head."

Finding now that I could get no further evidence ; that the information which I had already
obtained was considerable ;* and that the committee had expressed an earnest desire, in a letter
which I had received, that I would take into consideration the propriety of writing my Essay on
the Impolicy of the Slave-trade as soon as possible,
I determined upon leaving Liverpool.   I went
round accordingly and took leave of my friends.
The last of these was William Rathbone, and I
have to regret, that it was also the last time I ever
saw him.   Independently of the gratitude I owed
him for assisting me in this great cause, I respect-
ed him highly as a man.   He possessed a fine
understanding with a solid judgment.   He was
a person of extraordinary simplicity of manners.
Though he lived in a state of pecuniary indepen-
dence, he gave an example of great temperance,
as well as of great humility of mind.   But however humble he appeared, he had always the
courage to dare to do that which was right, however it might resist the customs or the prejudices
of men.   In his own line of trade, which was that
of a timber-merchant on an extensive scale, he

* In London, Bristol and Liverpool, I had already obtained the
names of more than 20,000 seamen, in different voyages, knowing
what had become of each.

would not allow any article to be sold for the use
of a slave-ship, and he always refused those, who
applied to him for materials for such purposes.
But it is evident that it was his intention, if he
had lived to bear his testimony still more publicly
upon this subject; for an advertisement, stating
the ground of his refusal to furnish any thing for
this traffic upon Christian principles, with a mem-
orandum for two advertisements in the Liverpool
papers, was found among his papers at his decease.

CHAPTER III.

AUTHOR PROCEEDS TO MANCHESTER—FINDS A SPIRIT RISING AMONG THE
PEOPLE THERE FOR THE ABOLITION OF THE SLAVE-TRADE—IS REQUEST-
ED TO DELIVER A DISCOURSE ON THE SUBJECT OF THE SLAVE-TRADE—
HEADS OF IT—AND EXTRACTS—PROCEEDS TO KEDDLESTON—AND BIR-
MINGHAM—FINDS A SIMILAR SPIRIT AT THE LATTER PLACE—REVISITS
BRISTOL—NEW AND DIFFICULT SITUATION THERE.—AUTHOR CROSSES
THE SEVERN AT NIGHT—UNSUCCESSFUL TERMINATION OF HIS JOURNEY
—RETURNS TO LONDON.

I now took my departure from Liverpool, and
proceeded to Manchester, where I arrived on the
Friday evening.   On the Saturday morning Mr.
Thomas Walker, attended by Mr. Cooper and
Mr. Bayley of Hope, called upon me.   They were
then strangers to me.   They came, they said,
having heard of my arrival, to congratulate me on
the spirit which was then beginning to show itself,
among the people of Manchester and of other
places, on the subject of the Slave-trade, and

which would unquestionably manifest itself further by breaking out into petitions to Parliament
for its abolition. I was much surprised at this
information. I had devoted myself so entirely to
my object, that I had never had time to read a
newspaper since I left London. I never knew
therefore, till now, that the attention of the public had been drawn to the subject in such a manner. And as to petitions, though I myself had
suggested the idea at Bridgewater, Bristol, Gloucester, and two or three other places, I had only
done it provisionally, and this without either the
knowledge or the consent of the committee. The
news, however, as it astonished, so it almost overpowered me with joy. I rejoiced in it because it
was a proof of the general good disposition of
my countrymen ; because it showed me that the
cause was such as needed only to be known, to
be patronised ; and because the manifestation of
this spirit seemed to me to be an earnest that
success would ultimately follow.

The gentlemen now mentioned took me away
with them, and introduced me to Mr. Thomas
Phillips. We conversed at first upon the discoveries made in my journey ; but in a little time,
understanding that I had been educated as a
clergyman, they came upon me with one voice,
as if it had been before agreed upon, to deliver a
discourse the next day, which was Sunday, on the
subject of the Slave-trade. I was always aware
that it was my duty to do all that I could with
propriety to serve the cause I had undertaken, and

yet I found myself embarrassed at their request. Foreseeing, as I have before related, that this cause might demand my attention to it for the greatest part of my life, I had given up all thoughts of my profession. I had hitherto but seldom exercised it, and then only to oblige some friend. I doubted too, at the first view of the thing, whether the pulpit ought to be made an engine for political purposes, though I could not but consider the Slave-trade as a mass of crimes, and therefore the effort to get rid of it as a Christian duty. I had an idea too, that sacred matters should not be entered upon without due consideration, nor prosecuted in a hasty, but in a decorous and solemn manner. I saw besides, that as it was then two o'clock in the afternoon, and this sermon was to be forthcoming the next day, there was not sufficient time to compose it properly. All these difficulties I suggested to my new friends without any reserve. But nothing that I could urge would satisfy them. They would not hear of a refusal, and I was obliged to give my consent, though I was not reconciled to the measure.

When I went into the church it was so full that I could scarcely get to my place; for notice had been publicly given, though I knew nothing of it, that such a discourse would be delivered. I was surprised also to find a great crowd of black people standing round the pulpit. There might be forty or fifty of them. The text that I took, as the best to be found in such a hurry, was the following: "Thou shalt not oppress a stranger,

4*

for ye know the heart of a stranger, seeing ye
were strangers in the land of Egypt."

I took an opportunity of showing from these
words, that Moses, in endeavoring to promote
among the children of Israel a tender disposition
towards those unfortunate strangers who had
come under their dominion, reminded them of
their own state when strangers in Egypt, as one
of the most forcible arguments which could be
used on such an occasion. For they could not
have forgotten that the Egyptians "had made
them serve with rigor; that they had made their
lives bitter with hard bondage, in mortar, and in
brick, and in all manner of service in the field;
and that all the service, wherein they made them
serve, was with rigor." The argument, therefore,
of Moses was simply this; "Ye knew well, when
ye were strangers in Egypt, the nature of your
own feelings. Were you not made miserable by
your debased situation there? But if so, you must
be sensible that the stranger, who has the same
heart, or the same feelings with yourselves, must
experience similar suffering, if treated in a similar
manner. I charge you then, knowing this, to
stand clear of the crime of his oppression."

The law then, by which Moses commanded
the children of Israel to regulate their conduct
with respect to the usage of the stranger, I showed to be a law of universal and eternal obligation,
and for this, among other reasons, that it was
neither more nor less than the Christian law,
which appeared afterwards, that we should not

do that to others, which we should be unwilling
to have done unto ourselves.

Having gone into these statements at some
length, I made an application of them in the following words :

"This being the case, and this law of Moses
being afterwards established into a fundamental
precept of Christianity, I must apply it to facts of
the present day, and I am sorry that I must apply
it to—ourselves.

"And first, Are there no strangers, whom we
oppress? I fear the wretched African will say,
that he drinks the cup of sorrow, and that he
drinks it at our hands. Torn from his native soil,
and from his family and friends, he is immediately
forced into a situation, of all others the most degrading, where he and his progeny are considered
as cattle, as possession, and as the possessions of
a man to whom he never gave offence.

"It is a melancholy fact, but it can be abundantly proved, that great numbers of the unfortunate strangers, who are carried from Africa to
our colonies, are fraudulently and forcibly taken
from their native soil. To descant but upon a
single instance of the kind must be productive of
pain to the ear of sensibility and freedom. Consider the sensations of the person, who is thus
carried off by the ruffians, who have been lurking
to intercept him. Separated from every thing
which he esteems in life, without the possibility
even of bidding his friends adieu, behold him over-
whelmed in tears; wringing his hands in despair;

looking backwards upon the spot where all his hopes and wishes lay, while his family at home are waiting for him with anxiety and suspense; are waiting, perhaps, for sustenance; are agitated between hope and fear; till length of absence confirms the latter, and they are immediately plunged into inconceivable misery and distress.

"If this instance, then, is sufficiently melancholy of itself, and is at all an act of oppression, how complicated will our guilt appear, who are the means of snatching away thousands annually in the same manner, and who force them and their families into the same unhappy situation, without either remorse or shame!"

Having proceeded to show, in a more particular manner than I can detail here, how, by means of the Slave-trade, we oppressed the stranger, I made an inquiry into the other branch of the subject, or how far we had a knowledge of his heart.

To elucidate this point, I mentioned several specific instances, out of those which I had collected in my journey, and which I could depend upon as authentic, of honor; gratitude; fidelity; filial, fraternal, and conjugal affection; and of the finest sensibility, on the part of those, who had been brought into our colonies from Africa, in the character of slaves, and when I proceeded for a while in the following words :—

"If, then, we oppress the stranger, as I have shown, and if, by a knowledge of his heart, we find that he is a person of the same passions and feelings as ourselves, we are certainly breaking, by means of the prosecution of the Slave-trade, that fundamental principle of Christianity, which says, that we shall not do that unto another, which we wish should not be done unto ourselves; and, I fear, cutting ourselves off from all expectation of the Divine blessing. For how inconsistent is our conduct! We come into the temple of God; we fall prostrate before him; we pray to him, that he will have mercy upon us. But how shall he have mercy upon us, who have had no mercy upon others! We pray to him, again, that he will deliver us from evil. But how shall he deliver us from evil, who are daily invading the rights of the injured African, and heaping misery on his head?"

I attempted, lastly, to show, that, though the sin of the Slave-trade had been hitherto a sin of ignorance, and might therefore have so far been winked at, yet as the crimes and miseries belonging to it became known, it would attach even to those who had no concern in it, if they suffered it to continue either without notice or reproach, or if they did not exert themselves in a reasonable manner for its suppression. I noticed, particularly, the case of Tyre and Sidon, which were the Bristol and the Liverpool of those times. A direct judgment had been pronounced by the prophet Joel against these cities, and, what is remarkable, for the prosecution of this same barbarous traffic. Thus, "And what have ye to do with me, O Tyre and Sidon, and all the coasts of Palestine? Ye have cast lots for my people. Ye have sold a girl for wine. The children of Judah, and the children of Jerusalem, have ye sold unto the Grecians, that ye might remove them far from their own border. Behold! I will raise them out of the place whither ye have sold them, and will recompense your wickedness on your own heads." Such was the language of the prophet; and Tyre and Sidon fell, as he had pointed out, when the inhabitants were either cut off, or carried into slavery.

Having thrown out these ideas to the notice of the audience, I concluded in the following words:—

"If, then, we wish to avert the heavy national judgment which is hanging over our heads (for must we not believe that our crimes towards the innocent Africans lie recorded against us in heaven) let us endeavor to assert their cause. Let us nobly withstand the torrent of the evil, however inveterately it may be fixed among the customs of the times; not, however, using our liberty as a cloak of maliciousness against those, who perhaps without due consideration have the misfortune to be concerned in it, but upon proper motives, and in a proper spirit, as the servants of God; so that if the sun should be turned into darkness, and the moon into blood, and the very heaven should fall upon us, we may fall in the general convulsion without dismay, conscious that we have done our duty in endeavoring to succor the distressed, and that the stain of the blood of Africa is not upon us."

From Manchester I proceeded to Keddleston in

Derbyshire, to spend a day with Lord Scarsdale, and to show him my little collection of African productions, and to inform him of my progress since I last saw him.' Here a letter was forwarded to me from the Reverend John Toogood, of Keinton Magna in Dorsetshire, though I was then unknown to him. He informed me that he had addressed several letters to the inhabitants of his own county, through their provincial paper, on the subject of the Slave-trade, which letters had produced a considerable effect. It appeared, however, that, when he began them, he did not know of the formation of our committee, or that he had a single coadjutor in the cause.

From Keddleston I turned off to Birmingham, being desirous of visiting Bristol in my way to London, to see if any thing new had occurred since I was there. I was introduced by letter, at Birmingham, to Sampson and Charles Lloyd, the brothers of John Lloyd, belonging to our committee, and members of the religious society of the Quakers. I was highly gratified in finding that these, in conjunction with Mr. Russell, had been attempting to awaken the attention of the inhabitants to this great subject, and that in consequence of their laudable efforts, a spirit was beginning to show itself there, as at Manchester, in favor of the abolition of the Slave-trade. The kind manner in which these received me, and the deep interest which they appeared to take in our cause, led me to an esteem for them, which, by means of subsequent visits, grew into a solid friendship.

At length I arrived at Bristol at about ten o'clock on Friday morning. But what was my surprise, when almost the first thing I heard from my friend Harry Gandy was, that a letter had been dispatched to me to Liverpool, nearly a week ago, requesting me immediately to repair to this place; for that in consequence of notice from the Lords of the Admiralty, advertised in the public papers, the trial of the chief mate, whom I had occasioned to be taken up at Bristol, for the murder of William Lines, was coming on at the Old Bailey, and that not an evidence was to be found. This intelligence almost paralyzed me. I cannot describe my feelings on receiving it. I reproached myself with my own obstinacy for having resisted the advice of Mr. Burges, as has been before explained. All his words now came fresh into my mind. I was terrified, too, with the apprehension that my own reputation was now at stake. I foresaw all the calumnies which would be spread, if the evidences were not forthcoming on this occasion. I anticipated, also, the injury which the cause itself might sustain, if, at our outset, as it were, I should not be able to substantiate what I had publicly advanced; and yet the mayor of Bristol had heard and determined the case; he had not only examined, but re-examined, the evidences; he had not only committed, but recommitted, the accused: this was the only consolation I had. I was sensible, however, amidst all these workings of my mind, that not a moment was to be lost, and I began, therefore, to set on foot an inquiry as to the absent persons.

On waiting upon the mother of William Lines, I learnt from her, that two out of four of the witnesses had been bribed by the slave-merchants, and sent to sea, that they might not be forthcoming at the time of the trial; that the two others had been tempted also, but that they had been enabled to resist the temptation; that, desirous of giving their testimony in this cause, they had gone into some coal-mine between Neath and Swansea, where they might support themselves till they should be called for; and that she had addressed a letter to them, at the request of Mr. Gandy, above a week ago, in which she had desired them to come to Bristol immediately, but that she had received no answer from them. She then concluded, either that her letter had miscarried, or that they had left the place.

I determined to lose no time, after the receipt of this intelligence; and I prevailed upon a young man, whom my friend Harry Gandy had recommended to me, to set off directly, and to go in search of them. He was to travel all night, and to bring them, or, if weary himself with his journey, to send them up, without ever sleeping on the road. It was now between twelve and one in the afternoon. I saw him depart. In the interim I went to Thompson's and other places, to inquire if any other of the seamen, belonging to the Thomas, were to be found: but, though I hunted diligently till four o'clock, I could learn nothing satisfactory.

I then went to dinner, but I grew uneasy. I was fearful that my messenger might be at a loss, or that he might want assistance on some occasion or other. I now judged that it would have been more prudent if two persons had been sent, who might have conferred with each other, and who might have divided, when they had reached Neath, and gone to different mines, to inquire for the witnesses. These thoughts disturbed me. Those, also, which had occurred when I first heard of the vexatious way in which things were situated, renewed themselves painfully to my mind. My own obstinacy in resisting the advice of Mr. Burges, and the fear of injury to my own reputation, and to that of the cause I had undertaken, were again before my eyes. I became still more uneasy; and I had no way of relieving my feelings, but by resolving to follow the young man, and to give him all the aid in my power.

It was now near six o'clock. The night was cold and rainy, and almost dark. I got down, however, safe to the passage-house, and desired to be conveyed across the Severn. The people in the house tried to dissuade me from my design. They said no one would accompany me, for it was quite a tempest. I replied, that I would pay those handsomely who would go with me. A person present asked me if I would give him three guineas for a boat, I replied I would. He could not for shame retract. He went out, and in about half an hour brought a person with him. We were obliged to have a lanthorn as far as the boat. We got on board, and went off. But such a passage I had never before witnessed. The wind was furious. The waves ran high. I could see nothing but white foam. The boat, also, was tossed up and down in such a manner that it was with great difficulty I could keep my seat. The rain, too, poured down in such torrents, that we were all of us presently wet through. We had been, I apprehend, more than an hour in this situation, when the boatmen began to complain of cold and weariness. I saw, also, that they began to be uneasy, for they did not know where they were. They had no way of forming any judgment about their course, but by knowing the point from whence the wind blew, and by keeping the boat in a relative position towards it. I encouraged them as well as I could, though I was beginning to be uneasy myself, and also sick. In about a quarter of an hour they began to complain again. They said they could pull no longer. They acknowledged, however, that they were getting nearer to the shore, though on what part of it, they could not tell. I could do nothing but bid them hope. They then began to reproach themselves for having come out with me. I told them I had not forced them, but that it was a matter of their own choice. In the midst of this conversation I informed them that I thought I saw either a star or a light straight forward. They both looked at it, and pronounced it to be a light, and added with great joy that it must be a light in the passage-house: and so we found it; for in about ten

minutes afterwards we landed, and, on reaching
the house, learnt that a servant maid had been
accidentally talking to some other persons on the
staircase, near a window, with a candle in her
hand, and that the light had appeared to us from
that circumstance.

It was now near eleven o'clock. My messenger,
it appeared, had arrived safe at about five in the
evening, and had proceeded on his route. I was
very cold on my arrival, and sick also. There
seemed to be a chilliness all over me, both within
and without. Indeed I had not a dry thread
about me. I took some hot brandy and water,
and went to bed; but desired, as soon as my
clothes were thoroughly dried, to be called up,
that I might go forward. This happened at about
two in the morning, when I got up. I took my
breakfast by the fireside. I then desired the post-
boy, if he should meet any persons on the road,
to stop, and inform me, as I did not know whether
the witnesses might not be coming up by themselves, and whether they might not have passed
my messenger without knowing his errand. Having taken these precautions, I departed. I travelled on, but we met no one. I traced, however,
my messenger through Newport, Cardiff, and
Cowbridge. I was assured, also, that he had not
passed me on his return; nor had any of those
passed me, whom he was seeking. At length,
when I was within about two miles of Neath, I
met him. He had both the witnesses under his
care. This was a matter of great joy to me. I

determined to return with them. It was now nearly two in the afternoon. I accordingly went back, but we did not reach the passage-house again till nearly two the next morning.

During our journey, neither the wind nor the rain had much abated. It was quite dark on our arrival. We found only one person, and he had been sitting up in expectation of us. It was in vain that I asked him for a boat to put us across the water. He said all the boatmen were in bed; and, if they were up, he was sure that none of them would venture out. It was thought a mercy by all of them, that we were not lost last night. Difficulties were also started about horses to take us another way. Unable therefore to proceed, we took refreshment and went to bed.

We arrived at Bristol between nine and ten the next morning; but I was so ill, that I could go no further; I had been cold and shivering ever since my first passage across the Severn, and I had now a violent sore throat, and a fever with it. All I could do was to see the witnesses off for London, and to assign them to the care of an attorney, who should conduct them to the trial. For this purpose I gave them a letter to a friend of the name of Langdale. I saw them depart. The mother of William Lines accompanied them. By a letter received on Tuesday, I learnt that they had not arrived in town till Monday morning at three o'clock; that at about nine or ten they found out the office of Mr. Langdale; that, on inquiring for him, they heard he was in the country, but

that he would be home at noon; that, finding he
had not then arrived, they acquainted his clerk
with the nature of their business, and opened my
letter to show him the contents of it; that the
clerk went with them to consult some other person on the subject, when he conveyed them to the
Old Bailey; but that, on inquiring at the proper
place about the introduction of the witnesses, he
learnt that the chief mate had been brought to the
bar in the morning, and, no person then appearing against him, that he had been discharged by
proclamation. Such was the end of all my anxiety
and labor in this affair. I was very ill when I
received the letter; but I saw the necessity of
bearing up against the disappointment, and I endeavored to discharge the subject from my mind
with the following wish, that the narrow escape
which the chief mate had experienced, and which
was entirely owing to the accidental circumstances now explained, might have the effect
under Providence, of producing in him a deep
contrition for his offence, and of awakening him
to a serious attention to his future life.*

I was obliged to remain in Bristol a few days
longer in consequence of my illness; but as soon
as I was able I reached London, when I attended
a sitting of the committee after an absence of more
than five months. At this committee it was

---

* He had undoubtedly a narrow escape, for Mr. Langdale's
clerk had learnt that he had no evidence to produce in his favor.
The slave-merchant, it seems, had counted most upon bribing those,
who were to come against him, to disappear.

strongly recommended to me to publish a second
edition of my Essay on the Slavery and Commerce of the Human Species, and to insert such
of the facts in it, in their proper places, out of
those collected in my late travels, as I might
judge to be productive of an interesting effect.
There appeared also an earnest desire in the committee, that, directly after this, I should begin my
Essay on the Impolicy of the Slave-trade.

In compliance with their wishes, I determined
upon both these works. But I resolved to retire
into the country, that, by being subject to less interruption there, I might the sooner finish them.
It was proper, however, that I should settle many
things in London, before I took my departure
from it; and, among these, that I should find out
George Ormond and Patrick Murray, whom I had
sent from Liverpool on account of the information
they had given me relative to the murder of Peter
Green. I saw no better way than to take them
before Sir Sampson Wright, who was then at the
head of the police of the metropolis. He examined, and cross-examined them several times, and
apart from each other. He then desired their
evidence to be drawn up in the form of depositions,
copies of which he gave to me. He had no doubt
that the murder would be proved. The circumstances of the deceased being in good health at
nine o'clock in the evening, and of his severe
sufferings till eleven, and of the nature of the
wounds discovered to have been made on his

person, and of his death by one in the morning,
could never, he said, be done away, by any evidence, who should state that he had been subject
to other disorders, which might have occasioned
his decease. He found himself therefore compelled to apply to the magistrates of Liverpool for
the apprehension of three of the principal officers
of the ship. But the answer was, that the ship
had sailed, and that they, whose names had been
specified, were then, none of them, to be found
in Liverpool.

It was now for me to consider, whether I would
keep the two witnesses, Ormond and Murray for
a year, or perhaps longer, at my own expense,
and run the hazard of the death of the officers in
the interim, and of other calculable events. I had
felt so deeply for the usage of the seamen in this
cruel traffic, which indeed had embittered all my
journey, that I had no less than nine prosecutions
at law upon my hands on their account, and nineteen witnesses detained at my own cost. The
committee in London could give me no assistance
in these cases. They were the managers of the
public purse for the abolition of the Slave-trade,
and any expenses of this kind were neither within
the limits of their object, nor within the pale
of their duty. From the individuals belonging to
it, I picked up a few guineas by way of private
subscription, and this was all. But a vast load
still remained upon me, and such as had occasioned uneasiness to my mind. I thought it there-

fore imprudent to detain the evidences for this
purpose for so long a time, and I sent them back
to Liverpool. I commenced, however, a prosecution against the captain at common law for his
barbarous usage of them, and desired that it might
be pushed on as vigorously as possible; and the
result was, that his attorney was so alarmed, particularly after knowing what had been done by
Sir Sampson Wright, that he entered into a compromise to pay all the expenses of the suit hitherto
incurred, and to give Ormond and Murray a sum
of money as damages for the injury which they
themselves had sustained. This compromise was
acceded to. The men received the money, and
signed the release, (of which I insisted upon a
copy,) and went to sea again in another trade,
thanking me for my interference in their behalf.
But by this copy, which I have now in my possession, it appears that care was taken by the
captain's attorney to render their future evidence
in the case of Peter Green, almost impracticable;
for it was there wickedly stated, "that George
Ormond and Patrick Murray did then and there
bind themselves in certain penalties, that they
would neither encourage nor support any action
at law against the said captain, by or at the suit
or prosecution of any other of the seamen now or
late on board the said ship, and that they released
the said captain also from all manner of actions,
suits, and cause and causes of action, informa-
tions, prosecutions and other proceedings, which

they then had, or ever had, or could or might
have by reason of the said assaults upon their own
persons, or *other wrongs or injuries done by the said
captain heretofore and to the date of this release.*"*

CHAPTER IV.

THE committee, during my absence, had attended regularly at their posts. They had been
both vigilant and industrious. They were, in
short, the persons, who had been the means of
raising the public spirit, which I had observed first
at Manchester, and afterwards as I journeyed on.
It will be proper, therefore, that I should now say
something of their labors, and of the fruits of
them. And if, in doing this, I should be more
minute for a few pages than some would wish, I
must apologize for myself by saying that there are
others, who would be sorry to lose the knowledge

* None of the nine actions before mentioned ever came to a
trial, but they were all compromised by paying sums to the injured
parties.

of the particular manner in which the foundation was laid, and the superstructure advanced, of a work, which will make so brilliant an appearance in our history as that of the abolition of the Slave-trade.

The committee having dispersed five hundred circular letters, giving an account of their institution, in London and its neighborhood, the Quakers were the first to notice it. This they did in their yearly epistle, of which the following is an extract: "We have also thankfully to believe there is a growing attention in many, not of our religious society, to the subject of negro slavery; and that the minds of the people are more and more enlarged to consider it as an aggregate of every species of evil, and to see the utter inconsistency of upholding it by the authority of any nation whatever, especially of such as punish, with loss of life, crimes whose magnitude bears scarce any proportion to this complicated iniquity."

The General Baptists were the next; for on the twenty-second of June, Stephen Lowdell and Dan Taylor attended as a deputation from the annual meeting of that religious body, to inform the committee, that those, whom they represented, approved their proceedings, and that they would countenance the object of their institution.

The first individual who addressed the committee was Mr. William Smith, the present member for Norwich. In his letter he expressed the pleasure he had received in finding persons associated in the support of a cause, in which he himself had taken a deep interest. He gave them advice as to their future plans. He promised them all the co-operation in his power : and he exhorted them not to despair, even if their first attempt should be unsuccessful ; " for consolation," says he, " will not be wanting. You may rest satisfied that the attempt will be productive of some good ; that the fervent wishes of the righteous will be on your side, and that the blessing of those who are ready to perish will fall upon you." And as Mr. Smith was the first person to address the committee as an individual after its formation, so, next to Mr. Wilberforce and the members of it, he gave the most time and attention to the promotion of the cause.

On the fifth of July, the committee opened a correspondence, by means of William Dillwyn, with the societies of Philadelphia and New York, of whose institution an account has been given. At this sitting a due sense was signified of the services of Mr. Ramsay, and a desire of his friendly communications when convenient.

The two next meetings were principally occu-pied in making out lists of the names of persons in the country, to whom the committee should send their publications for distribution. For this purpose every member was to bring in an account of those whom he knew personally, and whom he believed not only to be willing, but qualified on account of their judgment and the weight of their character, to take an useful part in the work, which was to be assigned to them. It is a remarkable circumstance, that, when the lists were arranged, the committee, few as they were, found they had friends in no less than thirty-nine counties,* in each of which there were several, so that a knowledge of their institution could now be soon diffusively spread.

The committee, having now fixed upon their correspondents, ordered five hundred of the circular letters, which have been before mentioned, and five thousand of the Summary Views, an account of which has been given also, to be printed.

On account of the increase of business, which was expected in consequence of the circulation of the preceding publications, Robert Barclay, John Vickris Taylor, and Josiah Wedgwood, esquire, were added to the committee; and it was then resolved, that any three members might call a meeting when necessary.

On the twenty-seventh of August, the new correspondents began to make their appearance. This sitting was distinguished by the receipt of letters from two celebrated persons. The first was from Brissot, dated Paris, August the eighteenth, who, it may be recollected, was an active member of the National Convention of France, and who suffered in the persecution of Robespierre.

---

* The Quakers by means of their discipline have a greater personal knowledge of each other than the members of any other religious society. But two-thirds of the committee were Quakers, and hence the circumstance is explained. Hence also nine-tenths of our first coadjutors were Quakers.

The second was from Mr. John Wesley, whose useful labors as a minister of the gospel are so well known to our countrymen.

Brissot, in this letter, congratulated the members of the committee, on having come together for so laudable an object. He offered his own assistance towards the promotion of it. He desired also that his valuable friend Claviere (who suffered also under Robespierre) might be joined to him, and that both might be acknowledged by the committee as associates in what he called this heavenly work. He purposed to translate and circulate through France, such publications as they might send him from time to time, and to appoint bankers in Paris, who might receive subscriptions and remit them to London for the good of their common cause. In the mean time, if his own countrymen should be found to take an interest in this great cause, it was not improbable that a committee might be formed in Paris, to endeavor to secure the attainment of the same object from the government in France.

The thanks of the committee were voted to Brissot for this disinterested offer of his services, and he was elected an honorary and corresponding member. In reply, however, to his letter it was stated, that, as the committee had no doubt of procuring from the generosity of their own nation sufficient funds for effecting the object of their institution, they declined the acceptance of any pecuniary aid from the people of France, but recommended him to attempt the formation of a committee in his own country, and to inform them of his progress, and, to make to them such other communications as he might deem necessary upon the subject from time to time.

Mr. Wesley, whose letter was read next, informed the committee of the great satisfaction which he also had experienced, when he heard of their formation. He conceived that their design, while it would destroy the Slave-trade, would also strike at the root of the shocking abomination of slavery also. He desired to forewarn them that they must expect difficulties and great opposition from those who were interested in the system; that these were a powerful body; and that they would raise all their forces, when they perceived their craft to be in danger. They would employ hireling writers, who would have neither justice nor mercy. But the committee were not to be dismayed by such treatment, nor even if some of those, who professed good-will towards them, should turn against them. As for himself, he would do all he could to promote the object of their institution. He would reprint a new and large edition of his Thought on Slavery, and circulate it among his friends in England and Ireland, to whom he would add a few words in favor of their design. And then he concluded in these words: "I commend you to Him, who is able to carry you through all opposition, and support you under all discouragements."

On the fourth, eleventh, and eighteenth of September, the committee were employed variously.

Among other things they voted their thanks to Mr. Leigh, a clergyman of the established church, for the offer of his services for the county of Norfolk. They ordered also one thousand of the circular letters to be additionally printed.

At one of these meetings a resolution was made, that Granville Sharp, esquire, be appointed chairman. This appointment, though now first formally made in the minute book, was always understood to have taken place; but the modesty of Mr. Sharp was such, that, though repeatedly pressed, he would never consent to take the chair, and he generally refrained from coming into the room till after he knew it to be taken. Nor could he be prevailed upon, even after this resolution, to alter his conduct: for though he continued to sign the papers, which were handed to him by virtue of holding this office, he never was once seated as the chairman during the twenty years in which he attended at these meetings. I thought it not improper to mention this trait in his character. Conscious that he engaged in the cause of his fellow-creatures solely upon the sense of his duty as a Christian, he seems to have supposed either that he had done nothing extraordinary to merit such a distinction, or to have been fearful lest the acceptance of it should bring a stain upon the motive, on which alone he undertook it.

On the second and sixteenth of October, two sittings took place; at the latter of which a sub-committee, which had been appointed for the purpose, brought in a design for a seal. An African was seen (as in the figure*) in chains in a supplicating posture, kneeling with one knee upon the ground,

and with both his hands lifted up to Heaven, and round the seal was observed the following motto, as if he was uttering the words himself, "Am I not a Man and a Brother?" The design having been approved of, a seal was ordered to be engraved from it. I may mention here, that this seal, simple as the design was, was made to contribute largely, as will be shown in its proper place, towards turning the attention of our countrymen to the case of the injured Africans, and of procuring a warm interest in their favor.

On the thirtieth of October several letters were read ; one of these was from Brissot and Claviere conjointly. In this they acknowledged the satisfaction they had received on being considered as associates in the humane work of the abolition of the Slave-trade, and correspondents in France for the promotion of it. They declared it to be their

---

* The figure is rather larger than that in the seal.

6 *

intention to attempt the establishment of a committee there on the same principles as that in
England : but, in consequence of the different constitutions of the two governments, they gave the
committee reason to suppose that their proceedings must be different, as well as slower than
those in England, for the same object.

A second letter was read from Mr. John Wesley.
He said that he had now read the publications,
which the committee had sent him, and that he
took, if possible, a still deeper interest in their
cause.   He exhorted them to more than ordinary
diligence and perseverance ; to be prepared for
opposition ; to be cautious about the manner of
procuring information and evidence, that no stain
might fall upon their character ; and to take care
that the question should be argued as well upon
the consideration of interest as of humanity and
justice, the former of which he feared would
have more weight than the latter ; and he recommended them and their glorious concern, as before, to the protection of Him who was able to
support them.

Letters were read from Dr. Price, approving
the institution of the committee ; from Charles
Lloyd of Birmingham, stating the interest which
the inhabitants of that town were taking in it;
and from William Russel, esquire, of the same
place, stating the same circumstance, and that
he would co-operate with the former in calling a
public meeting, and in doing whatever else was
necessary for the promotion of so good a cause.

A letter was read also from Manchester, signed conjointly by George Barton, Thomas Cooper, John Ferriar, Thomas Walker, Thomas Phillips, Thomas Butterworth Bayley, and George Lloyd, esquires, promising their assistance for that place. Two others were read from John Kerrich, esquire, of Harleston, and from Joshua Grigby, esquire, of Drinkston, each tendering their services, one for the county of Norfolk, and the other for the county of Suffolk. The latter concluded by saying, "With respect to myself, in no possible instance of my public conduct can I receive so much sincere satisfaction, as I shall by the vote I will most assuredly give in Parliament, in support of this most worthy effort to suppress a traffic, which is contrary to all the feelings of humanity, and the laws of our religion."

A letter was read also at this sitting from major Cartwright, of Marnham, in which he offered his own services, in conjunction with those of the reverend John Charlesworth, of Ossington, for the county of Nottingham.

"I congratulate you" says he in his letter, "on the happy prospect of some considerable step at least being taken towards the abolition of a traffic, which is not only impious in itself, but of all others tends most to vitiate the human mind.

"Although procrastination is generally pernicious in cases depending upon the feelings of the heart, I should almost fear that, without very uncommon exertions, you will scarcely be prepared early in the next sessions for bringing the business into Parliament with the greatest advantage. But be that as it may, let the best use be made of the intermediate time ; and then, if there be a super-intending Providence, which governs every thing in the moral world, there is every reason to hope for a blessing on this particular work."

The last letter was from Robert Boucher Nickolls, dean of Middleham in Yorkshire. In this he stated that he was a native of the West Indies, and had travelled on the continent of America. He then offered some important information to the committee, as his mite towards the abolition of the Slave-trade, and as an encouragement to them to persevere. He attempted to prove that the natural increase of the negroes already in the West Indian islands would be fully adequate to the cultivation of them without any fresh supplies from Africa, and that such natural increase would be secured by humane treatment. With this view he instanced the two estates of Mr. MacMahon and of Dr. Mapp in the island of Barbadoes. The first required continual supplies of new slaves, in consequence of the severe and cruel usage adopted upon it. The latter overflowed with laborers in consequence of a system of kindness, so that it almost peopled another estate. Having related these instances, he cited others in North America, where, though the climate was less favorable to the constitution of the Africans, but their treatment better, they increased also. He combated, from his own personal knowledge, the argument that self-interest was always sufficient to ensure good usage, and maintained that there was only one way of securing it, which was the entire abolition of the Slave-trade. He showed in what manner the latter measure would operate to the desired end. He then dilated on the injustice and inconsistency of this trade, and supported the policy of the abolition of it, both to the planter, the merchant, and the nation.

This letter of the Dean of Middleham, which was a little Essay of itself, was deemed of so much importance by the committee, but particularly as it was the result of local knowledge, that they not only passed a resolution of thanks to him for it, but desired his permission to print it.

The committee sat again on the thirteenth and twenty-second of November. At the first of these sittings, a letter was read from Henry Grimston, esquire, of Whitwell Hall, near York, offering his services for the promotion of the cause in his own county. At the second, the Dean of Middleham's answer was received. He acquiesced in the request of the committee ; when five thousand of his letters were ordered immediately to be printed.

On the twenty-second a letter was read from Mr. James Mackenzie, of the town of Cambridge, desiring to forward the object of the institution there. Two letters were read also, one from the late Mr. Jones, tutor of Trinity College, and the other from Mr. William Frend, fellow of Jesus College. It appeared from these that the gentlemen of the University of Cambridge were beginning

to take a lively interest in the abolition of the
Slave-trade, among whom Dr. Watson, the bishop
of Llandaff, was particularly conspicuous. At this
committee two thousand new Summary Views
were ordered to be printed, and the circular letter
to be prefixed to each.

CHAPTER V.

LABORS OF THE COMMITTEE CONTINUED TO FEBRUARY 1788.—COMMITTEE
ELECT NEW MEMBERS—VOTE THANKS TO FALCONBRIDGE AND OTHERS—
RECEIVE LETTERS FROM GROVE AND OTHERS—CIRCULATE NUMEROUS
PUBLICATIONS—MAKE A REPORT—SEND CIRCULAR LETTERS TO CORPO-
RATE BODIES—RELEASE NEGROES UNJUSTLY DETAINED—FIND NEW COR-
RESPONDENTS IN ARCHDEACON PALEY—THE MARQUIS DE LA FAYETTE—
BISHOP OF CLOYNE—BISHOP OF PETERBOROUGH—AND IN MANY OTHERS.

THE labors of the committee, during my absence, were as I have now explained them; but
as I was obliged, almost immediately on joining
them, to retire into the country to begin my new
work, I must give an account of their further services till I joined them again, or till the middle
of February 1788.

During sittings which were held from the middle of December, 1787, to the eighteenth of January, 1788, the business of the committee had so
increased, that it was found proper to make an
addition to their number. Accordingly James
Martin and William Morton Pitt, esquires, members of Parliament, and Robert Hunter, and Joseph
Smith, esquires, were chosen members of it.

The knowledge also of the institution of the society had spread to such an extent, and the eagerness among individuals to see the publications of the committee had been so great, that the press was kept almost constantly going during the time now mentioned. No fewer than three thousand lists of the subscribers, with a circular letter prefixed to them, explaining the object of the institution, were ordered to be printed within this period, to which are to be added fifteen hundred of Benezet's Account of Guinea, three thousand of the Dean of Middleham's Letters, five thousand Summary Views, and two thousand of a new edition of the Slavery and Commerce of the Human Species, which I had enlarged before the last of these sittings from materials collected in my late tour.

The thanks of the committee were voted during this period to Mr. Alexander Falconbridge, for the assistance he had given me in my inquiries into the nature of the Slave-trade.

As Mr. Falconbridge had but lately returned from Africa, and as facts and circumstances, which had taken place but a little time ago, were less liable to objections (inasmuch as they proved the present state of things) than those which had happened in earlier times, he was prevailed upon to write an account of what he had seen during the four voyages he had made to that continent; and accordingly, within the period which has been mentioned, he began his work.

The committee, during these sittings kept up

a correspondence with those gentlemen who were mentioned in the last chapter to have addressed them.   But, besides these, they found other voluntary correspondents in the following persons, Capel Lofft, esquire, of Troston, and the reverend R. Broome of Ipswich, both in the county of Suffolk.   These made an earnest tender of their services for those parts of the county in which they resided.   Similar offers were made by Mr. Hammond of Stanton, near St. Ives, in the county of Huntingdon, by Thomas Parker, esquire, of Beverley, and by William Grove, esquire, of Litchfield, for their respective towns and neighborhoods.

A letter was received also within this period from the society established at Philadelphia, accompanied with documents in proof of the good effects of the manumission of slaves, and with specimens of writing and drawing by the same. In this letter the society congratulated the committee in London on its formation, and professed its readiness to co-operate in any way in which it could be made useful.

During these sittings, a letter was also read from Dr. Bathurst, now bishop of Norwich, dated Oxford, December the seventeenth, in which he offered his services in the promotion of the cause.

Another was read, which stated that Dr. Horne, president of Magdalen College in the same university, and afterwards bishop of the same see as the former, highly favored it.

Another was read from Mr. Lambert, fellow of Trinity College, Cambridge, in which he signified

to the committee the great desire he had to promote the object of their institution. He had
drawn up a number of queries relative to the state
of the unhappy slaves in the islands, which he
had transmitted to a friend, who had resided in
them, to answer. These answers he purposed to
forward to the committee on their arrival.

Another was read from Dr. Hinchliffe, bishop
of Peterborough, in which he testified his hearty
approbation of the institution, and of the design
of it, and his determination to support the object
of it in Parliament. He gave in at the same time
a plan, which he called Thoughts on the Means
of Abolishing the Slave-trade in Great Britain and
in our West Indian islands, for the consideration
of the committee.

At the last of these sittings, the committee
thought it right to make a report to the public
relative to the state and progress of their cause;
but as this was composed from materials, which
the reader has now in his possession, it may not
be necessary to produce it.

On the twenty-second and twenty-ninth of January, and on the fifth and twelfth of February,
1788, sittings were also held. During these, the
business still increasing, John Maitland, esquire,
was elected a member of the committee.

As the correspondents of the committee were
now numerous, and as these solicited publications
for the use of those who applied to them, as well
as of those to whom they wished to give a knowledge of the subject, the press was kept in constant

employ during this period also. Five thousand two hundred and fifty additional Reports were ordered to be printed, and also three thousand of Falconbridge's Account of the Slave-trade, the manuscript of which was now finished. At this time, Mr. Newton, rector of St. Mary Woolnoth in London, who had been in his youth to the coast of Africa, but who had now become a serious and useful divine, felt it his duty to write his Thoughts on the African Slave-trade. The committee, having obtained permission, printed three thousand copies of these also.

During these sittings, the chairman was requested to have frequent communication with Dr. Porteus, bishop of London, as he had expressed his desire of becoming useful to the institution.

A circular letter also with the report before mentioned, was ordered to be sent to the mayors of several corporate towns.

A case also occurred, which it may not be improper to notice. The treasurer reported that he had been informed by the chairman, that the captain of the Albion merchant ship, trading to the Bay of Honduras, had picked up at sea from a Spanish ship which had been wrecked, two black men, one named Henry Martin Burrowes, a free native of Antigua, who had served in the royal navy, and the other named Antonio Berrat, a Spanish negro; that the said captain detained these men on board his ship, then lying in the river Thames, against their will; and that he would not give them up. Upon this report, it was resolved that the cause of these unfortunate captives should be espoused by the committee. Mr. Sharp accordingly caused a writ of habeas-corpus to be served upon them; soon after which he had the satisfaction of reporting, that they had been delivered from the place of their confinement.

During these sittings the following letters were read also:

One from Richard How, of Apsley, offering his services to the committee.

Another from the reverend Christopher Wyvill, of Burton Hall in Yorkshire, to the same effect.

Another from Archdeacon Plymley, (now Corbett,) in which he expressed the deep interest he took in this cause of humanity and freedom, and the desire he had of making himself useful as far as he could towards the support of it; and he wished to know, as the clergy of the diocese of Litchfield and Coventry were anxious to espouse it also, whether a petition to Parliament from them, as a part of the established church, would not be desirable at the present season.

Another from Archdeacon Paley, containing his sentiments on a plan for the abolition of the Slave-trade, and the manumission of slaves in our islands, and offering his future services, and wishing success to the undertaking.

Another from Dr. Sharp, prebendary of Durham, inquiring into the probable amount of the subscriptions which might be wanted, and for what purposes, with a view of serving the cause.

Another from Dr. Woodward, bishop of Cloyne, in which he approved of the institution of the committee. He conceived the Slave-trade to be no less disgraceful to the legislature and injurious to the true commercial interests of the country, than it was productive of unmerited misery to the unhappy objects of it, and repugnant both to the principles and the spirit of the Christian religion. He wished to be placed among the asserters of the liberty of his fellow-creatures, and he was therefore desirous of subscribing largely, as well as of doing all he could, both in England and Ireland, for the promotion of such a charitable work.

A communication was made, soon after the reading of the last letter, through the medium of the Chevalier de Ternant, from the celebrated Marquis de la Fayette of France. The marquis signified the singular pleasure he had received on hearing of the formation of a committee in England for the abolition of the Slave-trade, and the earnest desire he had to promote the object of it. With this view, he informed the committee that he should attempt the formation of a similar society in France. This he conceived to be one of the most effectual measures he could devise for securing the object in question; for he was of opinion, that if the two great nations of France and England were to unite in this humane and Christian work, the other European nations might be induced to follow the example.

The committee, on receiving the two latter communications, resolved, that the chairman should return their thanks to the Bishop of Cloyne, and the Marquis de la Fayette, and the Chevalier de Ternant, and that he should inform them, that they were enrolled among the honorary and corresponding members of the Society.

The other letters read during these sittings were to convey information to the committee, that people in various parts of the kingdom had then felt themselves so deeply interested in behalf of the injured Africans, that they had determined either on public meetings, or had come to resolutions, or had it in contemplation to petition Parliament, for the abolition of the Slave-trade. Information was signified to this effect by Thomas Walker, esquire, for Manchester; by John Hoyland, William Hoyles, esquire, and the reverend James Wilkinson, for Sheffield; by William Tuke, and William Burgh, esquire, for York; by the reverend Mr. Foster, for Colchester; by Joseph Harford and Edmund Griffith, esquires, for Bristol; by William Bishop, esquire, the mayor, for Maidstone; by the reverend R. Broome and the reverend J. Wright, for Ipswich; by James Clark, esquire, the mayor, for Coventry; by Mr. Jones, of Trinity College, for the University of Cambridge; by Dr. Schomberg, of Magdalen College, for the University of Oxford; by Henry Bullen, esquire, for Bury St. Edmunds; by Archdeacon Travis, for Chester; by Mr. Hammond, for the county of Huntingdon; by John Flint, esquire, (now Corbett) for the town of Shrewsbury and county

7*

of Salop; by the reverend Robert Lucast, for the
town and also for the county of Northampton;
by Mr. Winchester, for the county of Stafford;
by the reverend William Leigh, for the county of
Norfolk; by David Barclay, for the county of
Hertford; and by Thomas Babington, esquire, for
the county of Leicester.

CHAPTER VI.

FURTHER PROGRESS TO THE MIDDLE OF MAY.—PETITIONS BEGIN TO BE
SENT TO PARLIAMENT.—THE KING ORDERS THE PRIVY COUNCIL TO IN-
QUIRE INTO THE SLAVE-TRADE.—AUTHOR CALLED UP TO TOWN—HIS IN-
TERVIEWS WITH MR. PITT—AND WITH MR. (NOW LORD) GRENVILLE.—
LIVERPOOL DELEGATES EXAMINED FIRST—THEIR PREJUDICE THE COUN-
CIL—THIS PREJUDICE AT LENGTH COUNTERACTED.—LABORS OF THE
COMMITTEE IN THE INTERIM.—PUBLIC ANXIOUS FOR THE INTRODUCTION
OF THE QUESTION INTO PARLIAMENT.—MESSAGE OF MR. PITT TO THE
COMMITTEE CONCERNING IT—DAY FIXED FOR THE MOTION—SUBSTANCE
OF THE DEBATE WHICH FOLLOWED—DISCUSSION OF THE GENERAL QUES-
TION DEFERRED TILL THE NEXT SESSIONS.

BY this time the nature of the Slave-trade had,
in consequence of the labors of the committee and
of their several correspondents, become generally
known throughout the kingdom.   It had excited
a general attention, and there was among people a
general feeling in behalf of the wrongs of Africa.
This feeling had also, as may be collected from
what has been already mentioned, broken out into
language; for not only had the traffic become the
general subject of conversation, but public meetings had taken place, in which it had been dis-

cussed, and of which the result was, that an
application to Parliament had been resolved upon
in many places concerning it. By the middle
of February not fewer than thirty-five petitions
had been delivered to the commons, and it was
known that others were on their way to the same
house.

This ferment in the public mind, which had
shown itself in the public prints even before the
petitions had been resolved upon, had excited the
attention of government. To coincide with the
wishes of the people on this subject, appeared to
those in authority to be a desirable thing. To
abolish the trade, replete as it was with misery,
was desirable also : but it was so connected with
the interest of individuals, and so interwoven with
the commerce and revenue of the country, that
an hasty abolition of it without a previous inquiry appeared to them to be likely to be productive of as much misery as good. The king,
therefore, by an order of council, dated February
the eleventh, 1788, directed that a committee of
privy council should sit as a board of trade, " to
take into their consideration the present state of
the African trade, particularly as far as related to
the practice and manner of purchasing or obtaining slaves on the coast of Africa, and the importation and sale thereof, either in the British colonies and settlements, or in the foreign colonies
and settlements in America or the West Indies ;
and also as far as related to the effects and consequences of the trade both in Africa and in the

said colonies and settlements, and to the general commerce of this kingdom ; and that they should report to him in council the result of their inquiries, with such observations as they might have to offer thereupon."

Of this order of council Mr. Wilberforce, who had attended to this great subject, as far as his health would permit, since I left him, had received notice ; but he was then too ill himself to take any measures concerning it. He therefore wrote to me, and begged of me to repair to London immediately, in order to get such evidence ready as we might think it eligible to introduce when the council sat. At that time, as appears from the former chapter, I had finished the additions to my Essay on the Slavery and Commerce of the Human Species, and I had now proceeded about half way in that of the Impolicy of it. This summons, however, I obeyed, and returned to town on the fourteenth of February, from which day to the twenty-fourth of May, I shall now give the history of our proceedings.

My first business in London was to hold a conversation with Mr. Pitt previously to the meeting of the council, and to try to interest him, as the first minister of state, in our favor. For this purpose Mr. Wilberforce had opened the way for me, and an interview took place. We were in free conversation together for a considerable time, during which we went through most of the branches of the subject. Mr. Pitt appeared to me to have but little knowledge of it. He had

also his doubts, which he expressed openly, on
many points.   He was at a loss to conceive how
private interest should not always restrain the
master of the slave from abusing him. This
matter I explained to him as well as I could ; and
if he was not entirely satisfied with my interpre-
tation of it, he was at least induced to believe that
cruel practices were more probable than he had
imagined.   A second circumstance, the truth of
which he doubted, was the mortality and usage
of seamen in this trade; and a third was the statement, by which so much had been made of the
riches of Africa, and of the genius and abilities
of her people ; for he seemed at a loss to compre-
hend, if these things were so, how it had happened
that they should not have been more generally
noticed before.   I promised to satisfy him upon
these points, and an interview was fixed for this
purpose the next day.

At the time appointed I went with my books,
papers, and African productions.   Mr. Pitt examined the former himself.   He turned over leaf
after leaf, in which the copies of the muster-rolls
were contained, with great patience ; and when
he had looked over above a hundred pages accu-
rately, and found the name of every seaman inserted, his former abode or service, the time of his
entry, and what had become of him, either by
death, discharge or desertion, he expressed his
surprise at the great pains which had been taken
in this branch of the inquiry, and confessed,
with some emotion, that his doubts were wholly

removed with respect to the destructive nature
of this employ; and he said, moreover, that the
facts contained in these documents, if they had
been but fairly copied, could never be disproved.
He was equally astonished at the various woods
and other productions of Africa, but most of all at
the manufactures of the natives in cotton, leather,
gold and iron, which were laid before him. These
he handled and examined over and over again.
Many sublime thoughts seemed to rush in upon
him at once at the sight of these, some of which
he expressed with observations becoming a great
and dignified mind. He thanked me for the light
I had given him on many of the branches of this
great question. And I went away under a certain conviction that I had left him much impressed
in our favor.

My next visit was to Mr. (now lord) Grenville.
I called upon him at the request of Mr. Wilberforce, who had previously written to him from
Bath, as he had promised to attend the meetings
of the privy council during the examinations
which were to take place. I found in the course
of our conversation that Mr. Grenville had not
then more knowledge of the subject than Mr.
Pitt; but I found him differently circumstanced
in other respects, for I perceived in him a warm
feeling in behalf of the injured Africans, and that
he had no doubt of the possibility of all the barbarities which had been alleged against this traffic.
I showed him all my papers and some of my
natural productions, which he examined. I was

with him the next day, and once again afterwards, so that the subject was considered in all its parts. The effect of this interview with him was of course different from that upon the minister. In the former case I had removed doubts, and given birth to an interest in favor of our cause. But I had here only increased an interest which had already been excited. I had only enlarged the mass of feeling, or added zeal to zeal, or confirmed resolutions and reasonings. Disposed in this manner originally himself, and strengthened by the documents with which I had furnished him, Mr. Grenville contracted an enmity to the Slave-trade, which was never afterwards diminished.*

A report having gone abroad, that the committee of privy council would only examine those who were interested in the continuance of the trade, I found it necessary to call upon Mr. Pitt again, and to inform him of it, when I received an assurance that every person whom I chose to send to the council in behalf of the committee, should be heard. This gave rise to a conversation relative to those witnesses whom we had to produce on the side of the abolition. And here I was obliged to disclose our weakness in this respect. I owned with sorrow that, though I had

* I have not mentioned the difference between these two eminent persons, with a view of drawing any invidious comparisons, but because, as these statements are true, such persons as have a high opinion of the late Mr. Pitt's judgment, may see that this great man did not espouse the cause hastily, or merely as a matter of feeling, but upon the conviction of his own mind.

obtained specimens and official documents in abun-
dance to prove many important points; yet I had
found it difficult to prevail upon persons to be publicly examined on this subject. The only persons
we could then count upon, were Mr. Ramsay,
Mr. H. Gandy, Mr. Falconbridge, Mr. Newton,
and the Dean of Middleham. There was one,
however, who would be a host of himself, if we
could but gain him. I then mentioned Mr. Norris. I told Mr. Pitt the nature* and value of the
testimony which he had given me at Liverpool,
and the great zeal he had discovered to serve the
cause. I doubted, however, if he would come to
London for this purpose, even if I wrote to him;
for he was intimate with almost all the owners of
slave-vessels in Liverpool, and living among these
he would not like to incur their resentment, by
taking a prominent part against them. I therefore entreated Mr. Pitt to send him a summons of
council to attend, hoping that Mr. Norris would
then be pleased to come up, as he would be enabled to reply to his friends, that his appearance
had not been voluntary. Mr. Pitt, however, informed me, that a summons from a committee of
privy council sitting as a board of trade was not
binding upon the subject, and therefore that I had
no other means left but of writing to him, and he
desired me to do this by the first post.

This letter I accordingly wrote, and sent it to
my friend William Rathbone, who was to deliver

---

* See his evidence, Chap. I, Vol. II.

it in person, and to use his own influence at the
same time; but I received for answer, that Mr.
Norris was then in London.   Upon this I tried to
find him out, to entreat him to consent to an examination before the council.   At length I found
his address; but before I could see him, I was
told by the bishop of London, that he had come
up as a Liverpool delegate in support of the Slave-
trade.   Astonished at this information, I made
the bishop acquainted with the case, and asked
him how it became me to act; for I was fearful
lest, by exposing Mr. Norris, I should violate the
rights of hospitality on the one hand, and by not
exposing him, that I should not do my duty to the
cause I had undertaken on the other.   His advice
was, that I should see him, and ask him to explain the reasons of his conduct.   I called upon
him for this purpose, but he was out.   He sent
me, however, a letter soon afterwards, which was
full of flattery, and in which, after having paid
high compliments to the general force of my arguments and the general justice and humanity of
my sentiments on this great question, which had
made a deep impression upon his mind, he had
found occasion to differ from me, since we had
last parted, on particular points, and that he had
therefore less reluctantly yielded to the call of becoming a delegate; though notwithstanding he
would gladly have declined the office if he could
have done it with propriety.

At length the council began their examinations.
Mr. Norris, lieutenant Matthews, of the navy,

who had just left a slave-employ in Africa, and
Mr. James Penny, formerly a slave-captain, and
then interested as a merchant in the trade, (which
three were the delegates from Liverpool) took possession of the ground first. Mr. Miles, Mr. Weuves,
and others, followed them on the same side. The
evidence which they gave, as previously concerted
between themselves, may be shortly represented
thus :. They denied that kidnapping either did or
could take place in Africa, or that wars were made
there, for the purpose of procuring slaves. Having done away these wicked practices from their
system, they maintained positions which were less
exceptionable, or that the natives of Africa generally became slaves in consequence of having been
made prisoners in just wars, or in consequence of
their various crimes. They then gave a melancholy picture of the despotism and barbarity of
some of the African princes, among whom the
custom of sacrificing their own subjects prevailed.
But of all others, that which was afforded by Mr.
Norris on this ground was the most frightful. The
king of Dahomey, he said, sported with the lives
of his people in the most wanton manner. He
had seen at the gates of his palace, two piles of
heads like those of shot in an arsenal. Within
the palace the heads of persons newly put to death
were strewed at the distance of a few yards in the
passage which led to his apartment. This custom
of human sacrifice by the king of Dahomey was
not on one occasion only, but on many ; such as
on the reception of messengers from neighboring

states, or of white merchants, or on days of cere-
monial. But the great carnage was once a year,
when the poll-tax was paid by his subjects. A
thousand persons at least were sacrificed annually
on these different occasions. The great men,
too, of the country cut off a few heads on festival
days. From all these particulars the humanity
of the Slave-trade was inferred, because it took
away the inhabitants of Africa into lands where
no such barbarities were known. But the humanity of it was insisted upon by positive circumstances also, namely, that a great number of the
slaves were prisoners of war, and that in former
times all such were put to death, whereas now
they were saved ; so that there was a great acces-
sion of happiness to Africa since the introduction
of the trade.

These statements, and those of others on the
same side of the question, had a great effect, as
may easily be conceived, upon the feelings of those
of the council who were present. Some of them
began immediately to be prejudiced against us.
There were others who even thought that it was
almost unnecessary to proceed in the inquiry, for
that the trade was actually a blessing. They had
little doubt that all our assertions concerning it
would be found false. The bishop of London
himself was so impressed by these unexpected
accounts, that he asked me if Mr. Falconbridge,
whose pamphlet had been previously sent by the
committee to every member of the council, was
worthy of belief, and if he would substantiate

publicly what he had thus written. But these
impressions unfortunately were not confined to
those who had been present at the examinations.
These could not help communicating them to
others. Hence in all the higher circles (some of
which I sometimes used to frequent) I had the
mortification to hear of nothing but the Liverpool
evidence, and of our own credulity, and of the
impositions which had been practised upon us:
of these reports the planters and merchants did
not fail to avail themselves. They boasted that
they would soon do away all the idle tales which
had been invented against them. They desired
the public only to suspend their judgment till the
privy council report should be out, when they
would see the folly and wickedness of all our allegations. A little more evidence, and all would
be over. On the twenty-second of March, though
the committee of council had not then held its
sittings more than a month, and these only twice
or thrice a week, the following paragraph was seen
in a morning paper: " The report of the committee of privy council will be ready in a few days.
After due examination it appears that the major
part of the complaints against this trade are ill-
founded. Some regulations, however, are expected
to take place, which may serve in a certain degree
to appease the cause of humanity."

But while they who were interested had produced this outcry against us, in consequence of
what had fallen from their own witnesses in the
course of their examinations, they had increased

it considerably by the industrious circulation of a most artful pamphlet among persons of rank and fortune at the west end of the metropolis, which was called, Scriptural Researches on the Licitness of the Slave-trade. This they had procured to be written by R. Harris, who was then clerk in a slave-house in Liverpool, but had been formerly a clergyman and a Jesuit. As they had maintained in the first instance, as has been already shown, the humanity of the traffic, so, by means of this pamphlet they asserted its consistency with revealed religion. That such a book should have made converts in such an age is surprising; and yet many, who ought to have known better, were carried away by it; and we had now absolutely to contend, and almost to degrade ourselves by doing so, against the double argument of the humanity and the holiness of the trade.

By these means, but particularly by the former, the current of opinion in particular circles ran against us for the first month, and so strong, that it was impossible for us to stem it at once: but as some of the council recovered from their panic, and their good sense became less biased by their feelings, and they were in a state to hear reason, their prejudices began to subside. It began now to be understood among them, that almost all the witnesses were concerned in the continuance of the trade. It began to be known also, (for Mr. Pitt and the bishop of London took care that it should be circulated,) that Mr. Norris had but a short time before furnished me at Liverpool with

information, all of which he had concealed* from
the council, but all of which made for the abolition of it.   Mr. Devaynes also, a respectable member of Parliament, who had been in Africa, and
who had been appealed to by Mr. Norris, when
examined before the privy council, in behalf of his
extraordinary facts, was unable, when summoned,
to confirm them to the desired extent.   From this
evidence the council collected, that human sacrifices were not made on the arrival of white traders, as had been asserted; that there was no
poll-tax in Dahomey at all; and that Mr. Norris
must have been mistaken on these points, for he
must have been there at the time of the ceremony
of watering the graves, when about sixty persons
suffered.   This latter custom moreover appeared to
have been a religious superstition of the country,
such as at Otaheite, or in Britain in the time of
the Druids, and to have had nothing to do with
the Slave-trade.†   With respect to prisoners of
war, Mr. Devaynes allowed that the old, the lame,
and the wounded, were often put to death on the
spot; but this was to save the trouble of bringing
them away.   The young and the healthy were
driven off for sale; but if they were not sold
when offered, they were not killed, but reserved

---

* This was also the case with another witness, Mr. Weuves.
He had given me accounts, before any stir was made about the
Slave-trade, relative to it, all of which he kept back when he was
examined there.

† Being a religious custom, it would still have gone on, though
the Slave-trade had been abolished: nor could the merchants at
any time have brought off a single victim.

for another market, or became house-slaves to
the conquerors. Mr. Devaynes also maintained,
contrary to the allegations of the others, that a
great number of persons were kidnapped in order
to be sold to the ships, and that the government,
where this happened, was not strong enough to
prevent it. But besides these draw-backs from the
weight of the testimony which had been given,
it began to be perceived by some of the lords of
the council, that the cruel superstitions which
had been described, obtained only in one or two
countries in Africa, and these of insignificant extent ; whereas at the time, when their minds were
carried away as it were by their feelings, they had
supposed them to attach to the whole of that vast
continent. They perceived also, that there were
circumstances related in the evidence by the delegates themselves, by means of which, if they were
true, the inhumanity of the trade might be established, and this to their own disgrace. They had
all confessed that such slaves as the white traders
refused to buy were put to death ; and yet that
these traders, knowing that this would be the
case, had the barbarity uniformly to reject those
whom it did not suit them to purchase. Mr. Matthews had rejected one of this description himself,
whom he saw afterwards destroyed. Mr. Penny
had known the refuse thrown down Melimba rock.
Mr. Norris himself, when certain prisoners of war
were offered to him for sale, declined buying them
because they appeared unhealthy ; and though
the king then told him that he would put them

to death, he could not be prevailed upon to take them, but left them to their hard fate; and he had the boldness to state afterwards, that it was his belief that many of them actually suffered.

These considerations had the effect of diminishing the prejudices of some of the council on this great question: and when this was perceived to be the case, it was the opinion of·Mr. Pitt, Mr. Grenville, and the bishop of London, that we should send three or four of our own evidences for examination, who might help to restore matters to an equilibrium. Accordingly, Mr. Falconbridge, and some others, all of whom were to speak to the African part of the subject, were introduced. These produced a certain weight in the opposite scale. But soon after these had been examined, Dr. Andrew Sparman professor of physic, and inspector of the museum of the royal academy at Stockholm, and his companion, C. B. Wadstrom, chief director of the assay-office there, arrived in England. These gentlemen had been lately sent to Africa by the late king of Sweden, to make discoveries in botany, mineralogy, and other departments of science. For this purpose the Swedish ambassador at Paris had procured them permission from the French government to visit the countries bordering on the Senegal, and had ensured them protection there. They had been conveyed to the place of their destination, where they had remained from August, 1787, to the end of January, 1788; but meeting with obstacles which they had not foreseen, they had left it, and had returned to Havre-de-Grace, from whence they had just arrived in London, in their way home. It so happened, that by means of George Harrison, one of our committee, I fell in unexpectedly with these gentlemen. I had not long been with them before I perceived the great treasure I had found. They gave me many beautiful specimens of African produce. They showed me their journals, which they had regularly kept from day to day. In these I had the pleasure of seeing a number of circumstances minuted down, all relating to the Slave-trade, and even drawings on the same subject. I obtained a more accurate and satisfactory knowledge of the manners and customs of the Africans from these, than from all the persons put together whom I had yet seen. I was anxious, therefore, to take them before the committee of council, to which they were pleased to consent; and as Dr. Spaarman was to leave London in a few days, I procured him an introduction first. His evidence went to show, that the natives of Africa lived in a fruitful and luxuriant country, which supplied all their wants, and that they would be a happy people if it were not for the existence of the Slave-trade. He instanced wars which he knew to have been made by the Moors upon the negroes (for they were entered upon wholly at the instigation of the white traders) for the purpose of getting slaves, and he had the pain of seeing the unhappy captives brought in on such occasions, and some of them in a wounded state. Among them were many women and children, and the women were in great affliction. He saw also the king of Barbesin send out his parties on expeditions of a similar kind, and he saw them return with slaves. The king had been made intoxicated on purpose, by the French agents, or he would never have consented to the measure. He stated also, that in consequence of the temptations held out by slave-vessels coming upon the coast, the natives seized one another in the night, when they found opportunity; and even invited others to their houses, whom they treacherously detained, and sold at these times; so that every enormity was practised in Africa, in consequence of the existence of the trade. These specific instances made a proper impression upon the lords of the council in their turn: for Dr. Spaarman was a man of high character; he possessed the confidence of his sovereign; he had no interest whatever in giving his evidence on this subject, either on one or the other side; his means of information too had been large; he had also recorded the facts which had come before him, and he had his journal, written in the French language, to produce. The tide therefore, which had run so strongly against us, began now to turn a little in our favor.

While these examinations were going on, petitions continued to be sent to the House of Commons, from various parts of the kingdom. No less than one hundred and three were presented in this session. The city of London, though she was drawn the other way by the cries of commercial

interest, made a sacrifice to humanity and justice.
The two universities applauded her conduct by
their own example. Large manufacturing towns
and whole counties expressed their sentiments and
wishes in a similar manner. The Established
Church in separate dioceses, and the Quakers
and other dissenters, as separate religious bodies,
joined in one voice upon this occasion.

The committee in the interim were not unmind-
ful of the great work they had undertaken; and
they continued to forward it in its different departments. They kept up a communication by letter
with the most of the worthy persons who have
been mentioned to have written to them, but particularly with Brissot and Claviere, from whom
they had the satisfaction of learning, that a society
had at length been established at Paris for the
Abolition of the Slave-trade in France. The
learned Marquis de Condorcet had become the
president of it. The virtuous Duc de la Rochefoucauld, and the Marquis de la Fayette, had
sanctioned it by enrolling their names as the two
first members. Petion, who was placed afterwards
among the mayors of Paris, followed. Women
also were not thought unworthy of being honorary
and assistant members of this humane institution;
and among these were found the amiable Mar-
chioness of la Fayette, Madame de Poivre, widow
of the late intendant of the Isle of France, and
Madame Necker, wife of the first minister of state.

The new correspondents, who voluntarily offered their services to the committee during the first

part of the period now under consideration, were,
S. Whitcomb, Esq., of Gloucester; the reverend
D. Watson, of Middleton Tyas, Yorkshire; John
Murlin, Esq., of High Wycomb; Charles Collins,
Esq., of Swansea; Henry Tudor, Esq., of Shef-
field; the reverend John Hare of Lincoln; Samuel
Tooker, Esq., of Moorgate, near Rotherham; the
reverend G. Walker, and Francis Wakefield, Esq.,
of Nottingham; the reverend Mr. Hepworth, of
Burton-upon-Trent; the reverend H. Dannett, of
St. John's, Liverpool; the reverend Dr. Oglander,
of New College, Oxford; the reverend H. Coul-
thurst, of Sidney College, Cambridge; R. Selfe,
Esq., of Cirencester; Morris Birkbeck, of Han-
ford, Dorsetshire; William Jepson, of Lancaster;
B. Kaye, of Leeds; John Patison, Esq., of Pais-
ley; J. E. Dolben, Esq., of Northamptonshire; the
reverend Mr. Smith, of Wendover; John Wilkinson, Esq., of Woodford; Samuel Milford, Esq., of
Exeter; Peter Lunel, Esq., treasurer of the committee at Bristol; James Pemberton, of Philadelphia; and the president of the society at New
York.

The letters from new correspondents during the
latter part of this period were the following:—

One from Alexander Alison, Esq., of Edinburgh, in which he expressed it to be his duty to
attempt to awaken the inhabitants of Scotland to
a knowledge of the monstrous evil of the Slave-
trade, and to form a committee there to act in
union with that of London, in carrying the great
object of their institution into effect.

Another from Elhanan Winchester, offering the committee one hundred of his sermons, which he had preached against the Slave-trade, in Fairfax county in Virginia, so early as in the year 1774.

Another from Dr. Frossard, of Lyons; in which he offered his services for the south of France, and desired different publications to be sent him, that he might be better qualified to take a part in the promotion of the cause.

Another from professor Bruns, of Helmstadt in Germany, in which he desired to know the particulars relative to the institution of the committee, as many thousands upon the continent were then beginning to feel for the sufferings of the oppressed African race.

Another from reverend James Manning, of Exeter, in which he stated himself to be authorized by the dissenting ministers of Devon and Cornwall, to express their high approbation of the conduct of the committee, and to offer their services in the promotion of this great work of humanity and religion.

Another from William Senhouse, Esq., of the island of Barbadoes. In this he gave the particulars of two estates, one of them his own and the other belonging to a nobleman, upon each of which the slaves, in consequence of humane treatment, had increased by natural population only. Another effect of this humane treatment, had been, that these slaves were among the most orderly and tractable in that island. From these and other instances he argued, that if the planters would, all of them, take proper care of their slaves, their humanity would be repaid in a few years by a valuable increase in their property, and they would never want supplies from a traffic, which had been so justly condemned.

Two others, the one from Travers Hartley, and the other from Alexander Jaffray, esquires, both of Dublin, were read. These gentlemen sent certain resolutions, which had been agreed upon by the chamber of commerce and by the guild of merchants there relative to the abolition of the Slave-trade. They rejoiced in the name of those, whom they represented, that Ireland had been unspotted by a traffic, which they held in such deep abhorrence, and promised, if it should be abolished in England, to take the most active measures to prevent it from finding an asylum in the ports of that kingdom.

The letters of William Senhouse, and of Travers Hartley, and of Alexander Jaffray, esquires, were ordered to be presented to the committee of privy council, and copies of them to be left there.

The business of the committee having almost daily increased within this period, Dr. Baker, and Bennet Langton, esquire, who were the two first to assist me in my early labors, and who have been mentioned among the forerunners and coadjutors of the cause, were elected members of it. Dr. Kippis also was added to the list.

The honorary and corresponding members elected within the same period, were the Dean

of Middleham, T. W. Coke, esquire, member of
Parliament, of Holkham in Norfolk, and the reverend William Leigh, who has been before mentioned, of Little Plumstead in the same county.
The latter had published several valuable letters
in the public papers under the signature of Afri-
canus. These had excited great notice, and done
much good. The worthy author had now collected them into a publication, and had offered
the profits of it to the committee. Hence this
mark of their respect was conferred upon him.

The committee ordered a new edition of three
thousand of the Dean of Middleham's Letters to
be printed. Having approved of a manuscript
written by James Field Stanfield, a mariner, containing observations upon a voyage which he had
lately made to the coast of Africa for slaves, they
ordered three thousand of these to be printed also.
By this time the subject having been much talked
of, and many doubts and difficulties having been
thrown in the way of the abolition by persons interested in the continuance of the trade, Mr. Ramsay who has been often so honorably mentioned,
put down upon paper all the objections which
were then handed about, and also those answers
to each, which he was qualified from his superior
knowledge of the subject to suggest. This he
did, that the members of the legislature might
see the more intricate parts of the question unravelled; and that they might not be imposed
upon by the spurious arguments which were then
in circulation concerning it. Observing also the

poisonous effect which The Scriptural Researches on the Licitness of the Slave-trade had produced upon the minds of many, he wrote an answer on scriptural grounds to that pamphlet. These works were sent to the press, and three thousand copies of each of them were ordered to be struck off.

The committee in their arrangement of the distribution of their books, ordered Newton's Thoughts, and Ramsay's Objections and Answers, to be sent to each member of both houses of Parliament.

They appointed also three sub-committees for different purposes : one to draw up such facts and arguments respecting the Slave-trade, with a view of being translated into other languages, as should give foreigners a suitable knowledge of the subject ; another to prepare an answer to certain false reports which had been spread relative to the object of their institution, and to procure an insertion of it in the daily papers ; and a third to draw up rules for the government of the Society.

By the latter end of the month of March, there was an anxious expectation in the public, notwithstanding the privy council had taken up the subject, that some notice should be taken in the lower house of Parliament of the numerous petitions which had been presented there. There was the same expectation in many of the members of it themselves. Lord Penrhyn, one of the representatives for Liverpool, and a planter also, had anticipated this notice, by moving for such papers relative to ships employed, goods exported, produce imported, and duties upon the same, as would show the vast value of the trade, which it was in contemplation to abolish. But at this time Mr. Wilberforce was ill, and unable to gratify the expectations which had been thus apparent. The committee, therefore, who partook of the anxiety of the public, knew not what to do. They saw that two-thirds of the session had already passed. They saw no hope of Mr. Wilberforce's recovery for some time. Rumors too were afloat, that other members, of whose plans they knew nothing, and who might even make emancipation their object, would introduce the business into the house. Thus situated, they waited as patiently as they could till the eighth of April,* when they resolved to write to Mr. Wilberforce, to explain to him their fears and wishes, and to submit it to his consideration, whether, if he were unable himself, he would appoint some one, in whom he could confide, to make some motion in Parliament on the subject.

But the public expectation became now daily more visible. The inhabitants of Manchester, many of whom had signed the petition for that place, became impatient and they appointed Thomas Walker and Thomas Cooper, esquires, as their delegates, to proceed to London to communicate with the committee on this subject, to assist them in their deliberations upon it, and to give

* Brissot attended in person at this committee in his way to America, which it was then an object with him to visit.

9 *

their attendance while it was under discussion by the legislature.

At the time of the arrival of the delegates, who were received as such by the committee, a letter came from Bath, in which it was stated that Mr. Wilberforce's health was in such a precarious state, that his physicians dared not allow him to read any letter, which related to the subject of the Slave-trade.

The committee were now again at a loss how to act, when they were relieved from this doubtful situation by a message from Mr. Pitt, who desired a conference with their chairman. Mr. Sharp accordingly went and on his return made the following report: "He had a full opportunity," he said, "of explaining to Mr. Pitt that the desire of the committee went to the entire abolition of the Slave-trade. Mr. Pitt assured him that his heart was with the committee as to this object, and that he considered himself pledged to Mr. Wilberforce, that the cause should not sustain any injury from his indisposition; but at the same time observed, that the subject was of great political importance, and it was requisite to proceed in it with temper and prudence. He did not apprehend, as the examinations before the privy council would yet take up some time, that the subject could be fully investigated in the present session of Parliament; but said he would consider whether the forms of the house would admit of any measures, that would be obligatory on them to take it up early in the ensuing session."

In about a week after this conference, Mr. Morton Pitt was deputed by the minister to write to the committee, to say that he had found precedents for such a motion as he conceived to be proper, and that he would submit it to the House of Commons in a few days.

At the next meeting, which was on the sixth of May, and at which Major Cartwright and the Manchester delegates assisted, Mr. Morton Pitt attended as a member of the committee, and said that the minister had fixed his motion for the ninth. It was then resolved that deputations should be sent to some of the leading members of Parliament, to request their support of the approaching motion. I was included in one of these, and in that which was to wait upon Mr. Fox. We were received by him in a friendly manner. On putting the question to him, which related to the object of our mission, Mr. Fox paused for a little while, as if in the act of deliberation; when he assured us unequivocally, and in language which could not be misunderstood, that he would support the object of the committee to its fullest extent, being convinced that there was no remedy for the evil, but in the total abolition of the trade.

At length, the ninth, or the day fixed upon, arrived, when this important subject was to be mentioned in the House of Commons for the first time,*

* David Hartley made a motion some years before in the same house, as has been shown in a former part of this work, but this was only to establish a proposition, that the Slave-trade was contrary to the laws of God and the rights of man.

with a view to the public discussion of it. It is
impossible for me to give within the narrow limits
of this work all that was then said upon it ; and
yet as the debate, which ensued, was the first
which took place upon it, I should feel inexcus-
able if I were not to take some notice of it.

Mr. Pitt rose. He said he intended to move a
resolution relative to a subject, which was of more
importance than any which had ever been agitated
in that house. This honor he should not have
had, but for a circumstance, which he could not
but deeply regret, the severe indisposition of his
friend, Mr. Wilberforce, in whose hands every
measure, which belonged to justice, humanity and
the national interest, was peculiarly well placed.
The subject in question was no less than that of
the Slave-trade. It was obvious from the great
number of petitions, which had been presented
concerning it, how much it had engaged the public attention, and consequently how much it deserved the serious notice of that house, and how
much it became their duty to take some measure
concerning it. But whatever was done on such a
subject, every one would agree ought to be done
with the maturest deliberation. Two opinions
had prevailed without doors, as appeared from the
language of the different petitions. It had been
pretty generally thought that the African Slave-
trade ought to be abolished. There were others,
however, who thought that it only stood in need
of regulations. But all had agreed that it ought
not to remain as it stood at present. But that

measure, which it might be the most proper to
take, could only be discovered by a cool, patient,
and diligent examination of the subject in all its
circumstances, relations and consequences. This
had induced him to form an opinion, that the
present was not the proper time for discussing it;
for the session was now far advanced, and there
was also a want of proper materials for the full
information of the house. It would, he thought,
be better discussed, when it might produce some
useful debate, and when that inquiry, which had
been instituted by his majesty's ministers, (he
meant the examination by a committee of privy
council,) should be brought to such a state of
maturity, as to make it fit that the result of it
should be laid before the house. That inquiry,
he trusted, would facilitate their investigation,
and enable them the better to proceed to a decision,
which should be equally founded on principles of
humanity, justice and sound policy. As there
was not a probability of reaching so desirable an
end in the present state of the business, he meant
to move a resolution to pledge the house to the
discussion of the question early in the next session. If by that time his honorable friend should
be recovered, which he hoped would be the case,
then he (Mr. Wilberforce) would take the lead in
it; but should it unfortunately happen otherwise,
then he (the chancellor of the exchequer) pledged
himself to bring forward some proposition concerning it. The house, however, would observe,
that he had studiously avoided giving any opinion

of his own on this great subject. He thought it
wiser to defer this till the time of the discussion
should arrive. He concluded with moving after
having read the names of the places from whence
the different petitions had come, "That this house
will, early in the next session of Parliament proceed to take into consideration the circumstances .
of the Slave-trade complained of in the said peti-.
tions, and what may be fit to be done thereupon."

Mr. Fox began by observing, that he had long
taken an interest in this great subject, which he
had also minutely examined, and that it was his
intention to have brought something forward himself in Parliament respecting it: but when he
heard that Mr. Wilberforce had resolved to take
it up, he was unaffectedly rejoiced, not only knowing the purity of his principles and character, but
because, from a variety of considerations as to
the situations in which different men stood in
the house, there was something that made him
honestly think it was better that the business·
should be in the hands of that gentleman, than in
his own. Having premised this, he said that, as,
so many petitions, and these signed by such numbers of persons of the most respectable character,
had been presented, he was sorry that it had been
found impossible that the subject of them could
be taken up this year and more particularly as he
was not able to see, as the chancellor of the exchequer had done, that there were circumstances,
which might happen by the next year, which
would make it more advisable and advantageous

to take it up then, than it would have been to
. enter upon it in the present session. For certainly
there could be no information laid before the
house, through the medium of the lords of the
council, which could not more advantageously
have been obtained by themselves, had they instituted a similar inquiry.   It was their duty to
advise the king, and not to ask his advice.   This
the constitution had laid down as one of its most
essential principles; and though in the present
instance he saw no cause for blame, because he
was persuaded his majesty's ministers had not
acted with any ill intention, it was still a principle
never to be departed from, because it never could
be departed from without establishing a precedent
which might lead to very serious abuses.   He
lamented that the privy council, who had received
no petitions from the people on the subject, should
have instituted an inquiry, and that the House
of Commons, the table of which had been loaded
with petitions from various parts of the kingdom,
should not have instituted any inquiry at all.   He
hoped these petitions would have a fair discussion
in that house, independently of any information
that could be given to it by his majesty's ministers.
He urged again the superior advantages of an inquiry into such a subject, carried on within those
walls, over any inquiry carried on by the lords of
the council.   In inquiries carried on in that house,
they had the benefit of every circumstance of pub-
licity ; which was a most material benefit indeed,
and that which of all others made the manner of

conducting the parliamentary proceedings of Great
Britain the envy and the admiration of the world.
An inquiry there was better than an inquiry in any
other place, however respectable the persons before and by whom it was carried on. There, all
that could be said for the abolition or against it
might be said. In that house, every relative fact
would have been produced, no information would
have been withheld, no circumstances would have
been omitted, which was necessary for elucidation ; nothing would have been kept back. He
was sorry therefore that the consideration of the
question, but more particularly where so much
human suffering was concerned, should be put
off to another session, when it was obvious that no
advantage could be gained by the delay.

He then adverted to the secrecy, which the
chancellor of the exchequer had observed relative
to his own opinion on this important subject. Why
did he refuse to give it ? Had Mr. Wilberforce
been present, the house would have had a great
advantage in this respect, because doubtless he
would have stated in what view he saw the subject, and in a general way described the nature
of the project he meant to propose. But now they
were kept in the dark as to the nature of any
plan, till the next session. The chancellor of the
exchequer had indeed said, that it had been a
very general opinion that the African Slave-trade
should be abolished. He had said again, that
others had not gone so far, but had given it as
their opinion, that it required to be revised and

regulated. But why did he not give his own sentiments boldly to the world on this great question?
As for himself, he (Mr. Fox) had no scruple to
declare at the outset, that the Slave-trade ought
not to be regulated, but destroyed. To this opinion
his mind was made up; and he was persuaded
that, the more the subject was considered, the
more his opinion would gain ground: and it would
be admitted, that to consider it in any other manner, or on any other principles than those of humanity and justice, would be idle and absurd.
If there were any such men, and he did not know
but that there were those, who, led away by local
and interested considerations, thought the Slave-
trade might still continue under certain modifications, these were the dupes of error; and mistook
what they thought their interest, for what he
would unedrtake to convince them was their loss.
Let such men only hear the case further, and they
would find the result to be, that a cold-hearted
policy was folly, when it opposed the great principles of humanity and justice.

He concluded by saying that he would not
oppose the resolution, if other members thought it
best to postpone the consideration of the subject;
but he should have been better pleased, if it had
been discussed sooner; and he certainly reserved
to himself the right of voting for any question
upon it that should be brought forward by any
other member in the course of the present session.

The chancellor of the exchequer said, that
nothing he had heard had satisfied him of the

propriety of departing from the rule he had laid.
down for himself, of not offering, but of studiously
avoiding to offer, any opinion upon the subject
till the time should arrive when it could be fully
argued. He thought that no discussion, which
could take place that session, could lead to any
useful measure, and therefore he had wished not
to argue it till the whole of it could be argued.
A day would come, when every member would
have an opportunity of stating his opinion; and
he wished it might be discussed with a proper
spirit on all sides, on fair and liberal principles,
and without any shackles from local and interested considerations.

With regard to the inquiries instituted before
the committee of privy council, he was sure, as
soon as it became obvious that the subject must
undergo a discussion, it was the duty of his majesty's ministers to set those inquiries on foot,
which should best enable them to judge in what
manner they could meet or offer any proposition
respecting the Slave-trade. And although such
previous examinations by no means went to de-
prive that house of its undoubted right to institute
those inquiries, or to preclude them, they would
be found greatly to facilitate them. But, exclu-
sive of this consideration, it would have been
utterly impossible to have come to any discussion
of the subject, that could have been brought to a
conclusion in the course of the present session.
Did the inquiry then before the privy council
prove a loss of time? So far from it, that, upon

the whole, time had been gained by it. He had
moved the resolution, therefore, to pledge the house
to bring on the discussion early in the next session,
when they would have a full opportunity of considering every part of the subject : first, Whether
the whole of the trade ought to be abolished ; and,
if so, how and when. If it should be thought
that the trade should only be put under certain
regulations, what those regulations ought to be,
and when they should take place. These were
questions which must be considered ; and therefore he had made his resolution as wide as possible, that there might be room for all necessary
considerations to be taken in. He repeated his
declaration, that he would reserve his sentiments
till the day of discussion should arrive ; and again
declared, that he earnestly wished to avoid an
anticipation of the debate upon the subject. But
if such debate was likely to take place, he would
withraw his motion, and offer it another day.

A few words then passed between Mr. Pitt and
Mr. Fox in reply to each other ; after which lord
Penrhyn rose. He said there were two classes of
men, the African merchants, and the planters,
both whose characters had been grossly calumniated. These wished that an inquiry might be
instituted, and this immediately, conscious that
the more their conduct was examined the less they
would be found to merit the opprobrium with
which they had been loaded. The charges against
the Slave-trade were either true or false. If they
were true, it ought to be abolished ; but if upon

inquiry they were found to be without foundation, justice ought to be done to the reputation of those who were concerned in it. He then said a few words, by which he signified, that, after all, it might not be an improper measure to make regulations in the trade.

Mr. Burke said, the noble lord, who was a man of honor himself, had reasoned from his own conduct, and being conscious of his own integrity, was naturally led to imagine that other men were equally just and honorable. Undoubtedly the merchants and planters had a right to call for an investigation of their conduct, and their doing so did them great credit. The Slave-trade also ought equally to be inquired into. Neither did he deny that it was right his majesty's ministers should inquire into its merits for themselves. They had done their duty; but that house, who had the petitions of the people on their table, had neglected it, by having so long deferred an inquiry of their own. If that house wished to preserve their functions, their understandings, their honor, and their dignity, he advised them to beware of committees of privy council. If they suffered their business to be done by such means, they were abdicating their trust and character, and making way for an entire abolition of their functions, which they were parting with one after another. Thus

Star after star goes out, and all is night.

If they neglected the petitions of their constituents, they must fall, and the privy council be

instituted in their stead. What would be the consequence? His majesty's ministers, instead of consulting them, and giving them the opportunity of
exercising their functions of deliberation and legislation, would modify the measures of government
elsewhere, and bring down the edicts of the privy
council to them to register.   Mr. Burke said, he
was one of those who wished for the abolition of
the Slave-trade. He thought it ought to be abolished, on principles of humanity and justice. If,
however, opposition of interests should render its
total abolition impossible, it ought to be regulated,
and that immediately. They need not send to the
West Indies to know the opinions of the planters
on the subject. They were to consider first of all,
and abstractedly from all political, personal, and
local considerations, that the Slave-trade was directly contrary to the principles of humanity and
justice, and to the spirit of the British constitution ; and that the state of slavery, which followed
it, however mitigated, was a state so improper,
so degrading, and so ruinous to the feelings and
capacities of human nature, that it ought not to
be suffered to exist.   He deprecated delay in this
business, as well for the sake of the planters as
of the slaves.

Mr. Gascoyne, the other member for Liverpool,
said he had no objection that the discussion should
stand over to the next session of Parliament, provided it could not come on in the present, because
he was persuaded it would ultimately be found
that his constituents, who were more immediately

concerned in the trade, and who had been so
shamefully calumniated, were men of respectable
character. He hoped the privy council would
print their report when they had brought their
inquiries to a conclusion, and that they would
lay it before the house and the public, in order to
enable all concerned to form a judgment of what
was proper to be done relative to the subject, next
session. With respect, however to the total abolition of the Slave-trade, he must confess that such
a measure was both unnecessary, visionary, and
impracticable; but he wished some alterations or
modifications to be adopted. He hoped that,
when the house came to go into the general question, they would not forget the trade, commerce,
and navigation of the country.

Mr. Rolle said, he had received instructions
from his constituents to inquire if the grievances,
which had been alleged to result from the Slave-
trade, were well founded, and, if it should appear
that they were, to assist in applying a remedy.
He was glad the discussion had been put off till
next session, as it would give all of them an opportunity of considering the subject with more
mature deliberation.

Mr. Martin desired to say a few words only.
He put the case, that, supposing the slaves were
treated ever so humanely, when they were carried
to the West Indies, what compensation could be
made them for being torn from their nearest relations, and from every thing that was dear to
them in life? He hoped no political advantage,

no national expediency, would be allowed to weigh
in the scale against the eternal rules of moral rec-
titude.   As for himself, he had no hesitation to
declare, in this early stage of the business, that
he should think himself a wicked wretch if he
did not do every thing in his power to put a stop
to the Slave-trade.

Sir William Dolben said, that he did not then
wish to enter into the discussion of the general
question of the abolition of the Slave-trade, which
the chancellor of the exchequer was so desirous
of postponing; but he wished to say a few words
on what he conceived to be a most crying evil,
and which might be immediately remedied, without infringing upon the limits of that question.
He did not allude to the sufferings of the poor
Africans in their own country, nor afterwards in
the West India islands, but to that intermediate
state of tenfold misery which they underwent in
their transportation. When put on board the ships,
the poor unhappy wretches were chained to each
other, hand and foot, and stowed so close, that
they were not allowed above a foot and a half for
each individual in breadth.   Thus crammed together like herrings in a barrel, they contracted
putrid and fatal disorders; so that they who came
to inspect them in a morning, had occasionally to
pick dead slaves out of their rows, and to unchain
their carcasses from the bodies of their wretched
fellow-sufferers, to whom they had been fastened.
Nor was it merely to the slaves that the baneful
effects of the contagion thus created were confined.

This contagion affected the ships' crews, and numbers of the seamen employed in the horrid traffic perished. This evil, he said, called aloud for a remedy, and that remedy ought to be applied soon, otherwise no less than ten thousand lives might be lost between this and the next session. He wished therefore this grievance to be taken into consideration, independently of the general question; and that some regulations, such as restraining the captains from taking above a certain number of slaves on board, according to the size of their vessels, and obliging them to let in fresh air, and provide better accommodation for the slaves during their passage, should be adopted.

Mr. Young wished the consideration of the whole subject to stand over to the next session.

Sir James Johnstone, though a planter, professed himself a friend to the abolition of the Slave-trade. He said it was highly necessary that the house should do something respecting it; but whatever was to be done should be done soon, as delay might be productive of bad consequences in the islands.

Mr. L. Smith stood up a zealous advocate for the abolition of the Slave-trade. He said that even lord Penrhyn and Mr. Gascoyne, the members for Liverpool, had admitted the evil of it to a certain extent; for regulations or modifications, in which they seemed to acquiesce, were unnecessary where abuses did not really exist.

Mr. Grigby thought it his duty to declare, that no privy council report, or other mode of

examination, could influence him.   A traffic in the
persons of men was so odious, that it ought every
where, as soon as ever it was discovered, to be
abolished.

Mr. Bastard was anxious that the house should
proceed to the discussion of the subject in the
present session.   The whole country, he said,
had petitioned ; and was it any satisfaction to the
country to be told, that the committee of privy
council were inquiring ?   Who knew any thing of
what was doing by the committee of privy council,
or what progress they were making ?   The inquiry
ought to have been instituted in that house, and
in the face of the public, that every body concerned might know what was going on.   The
numerous petitions of the people ought immediately to be attended to.   He reprobated delay on
this occasion ; and as the honorable baronet, Sir
William Dolben, had stated facts which were
shocking to humanity, he hoped he would move
that a committee might be appointed to inquire
into their existence, that a remedy might be applied, if possible, before the sailing of the next
ships for Africa.

Mr. Whitbread professed himself a strenuous
advocate for the total and immediate abolition
of the Slave-trade.   It was contrary to nature,
and to every principle of justice, humanity, and
religion.

Mr. Pelham stated, that he had very maturely
considered the subject of the Slave-trade ; and had
he not known that the business was in the hands

of an honorable member (whose absence from the
house, and the cause of it, no man lamented
more sincerely than he did) he should have ventured to propose something concerning it himself.
If it should be thought that the trade ought not
to be entirely done away, the sooner it was regulated the better.   He had a plan for this purpose,
which appeared to him to be likely to produce
some salutary effects.   He wished to know if any
such thing would be permitted to be proposed in
the course of the present session.

The chancellor of the exchequer said he should
be happy, if he thought the circumstances of the
house were such as to enable them to proceed to
an immediate discussion of the question ; but as
that did not appear, from the reasons he had
before stated, to be the case, he could only assure
the honorable gentleman, that the same motives
which had induced him to propose an inquiry into
the subject early in the next session of Parliament,
would make him desirous of receiving any other
light which could be thrown upon it.

The question having been then put, the resolution was agreed to unanimously.   Thus ended the
first debate that ever took place in the commons,
on this important subject.   This debate, though
many of the persons concerned in it abstained cau-
tiously from entering into the merits of the general question, became interesting, in consequence
of circumstances attending it.   Several rose up at
once to give relief, as it were to their feelings by
utterance ; but by so doing they were prevented,

many of them, from being heard. They who were
heard spoke with peculiar energy, as if warmed in
an extraordinary manner by the subject. There
was an apparent enthusiasm in behalf of the
injured Africans. It was supposed by some, that
there was a moment, in which, if the chancellor
of the exchequer had moved for an immediate
abolition of the trade, he would have carried it
that night; and both he and others, who professed
an attachment to the cause, were censured for not
having taken a due advantage of the disposition
which was so apparent. But independently of
the inconsistency of doing this on the part of the
ministry, while the privy council were in the
midst of their inquiries, and of the improbability
that the other branches of the legislature would
have concurred in so hasty a measure ; what good
would have accrued to the cause, if the abolition
had been then carried ? Those concerned in the
cruel system would never have rested quietly
under the stigma under which they then labored.
They would have urged, that they had been condemned unheard. The merchants would have
said, that they had had no notice of such an event,
that they might prepare a way for their vessels in
other trades. The planters would have said, that
they had had no time allowed them to provide
such supplies from Africa as might enable them
to keep up their respective stocks. They would,
both of them, have called aloud for immediate
indemnification. They would have decried the
policy of the measure of the abolition ; and where

had it been proved? They would have demanded
a reverse of it; and might they not, in cooler mo-
ments, have succeeded? Whereas, by entering
into a patient discussion of the merits of the question; by bringing evidence upon it; by reasoning
upon that evidence night after night, and year
after year, and thus by disputing the ground inch
as it were by inch, the abolition of the Slave-trade
stands upon a rock, upon which it never can be
shaken. Many of those who were concerned in the
cruel system have now given up their prejudices,
because they became convinced in the contest.
A stigma too has been fixed upon it, which can
never be erased: and in a large record, in which
the cruelty and injustice of it have been recognised in indelible characters, its impolicy also has
been eternally enrolled.

CHAPTER VII.

CONTINUATION TO THE MIDDLE OF JULY.—ANXIETY OF SIR WILLIAM
DOLBEN TO LESSEN THE HORRORS OF THE MIDDLE PASSAGE TILL THE
GREAT QUESTION SHOULD BE DISCUSSED—BRINGS IN A BILL FOR THAT
PURPOSE—DEBATE UPON IT—EVIDENCE EXAMINED AGAINST IT—ITS
INCONSISTENCY AND FALSEHOODS—FURTHER DEBATE UPON IT—BILLS
PASSED, AND CARRIED TO THE LORDS—VEXATIOUS DELAYS AND OPPOSI-
TION THERE—CARRIED BACKWARDS AND FORWARDS TO BOTH HOUSES—
AT LENGTH FINALLY PASSED.—PROCEEDINGS OF THE COMMITTEE IN
THE INTERIM—EFFECTS OF THEM.

IT was supposed, after the debate, of which the
substance has been just given, that there would
have been no further discussion of the subject till
the next year: but Sir William Dolben became
more and more affected by those considerations
which he had offered to the house on the ninth
of May. The trade, he found, was still to go on.
The horrors of the transportation, or middle passage, as it was called, which he conceived to be
the worst in the long catalogue of evils belonging to the system, would of course accompany it.
The partial discussion of these, he believed, would
be no infringement of the late resolution of the
house. He was desirous, therefore, of doing
something in the course of the present session, by
which the miseries of the trade might be diminished as much as possible, while it lasted, or till
the legislature could take up the whole of the
question. This desire he mentioned to several of
his friends; and as these approved of his design,

he made it known on the twenty-first of May in
the House of Commons.

He began by observing, that he would take up
but little of their time. He rose to move for
leave to bring in a bill for the relief of those unhappy persons, the natives of Africa, from the
hardships to which they were usually exposed in
their passage from the coast of Africa to the colonies. He did not mean, by any regulations he
might introduce for this purpose, to countenance
or sanction the Slave-trade, which, however mod-
ified, would be always wicked and unjustifiable.
Nor did he mean, by introducing these, to go into
the general question which the house had prohibited. The bill which he had in contemplation,
went only to limit the number of persons to be
put on board to the tonnage of the vessel which
was to carry them, in order to prevent them from
being crowded too closely together; to secure to
them good and sufficient provisions; and to take
cognizance of other matters, which related to their
health and accommodation; and this only till
Parliament could enter into the general merits
of the question. This humane interference he
thought no member would object to. Indeed,
those for Liverpool had both of them admitted, on
the ninth of May, that regulations were desirable;
and he had since conversed with them, and was
happy to learn that they would not oppose him
on this occasion.

Mr. Whitbread highly approved of the object
of the worthy baronet, which was to diminish the

sufferings of an unoffending people. Whatever could be done to relieve them in their hard situation, till Parliament could take up the whole of their case, ought to be done by men living in a civilized country, and professing the Christian religion: he therefore begged leave to second the motion which had been made.

General Norton was sorry that he had not risen up sooner. He wished to have seconded this humane motion himself. It had his most cordial approbation.

Mr. Burgess complimented the worthy baronet on the honor he had done himself on this occasion, and congratulated the house on the good which they were likely to do by acceding, as he was sure they would, to his proposition.

Mr. Joliffe rose, and said that the motion in question should have his strenuous support.

Mr. Gascoyne stated, that having understood from the honorable baronet that he meant only to remedy the evils, which were stated to exist in transporting the inhabitants of Africa to the West Indies, he had told him that he would not object to the introduction of such a bill. Should it however interfere with the general question, the discussion of which had been prohibited, he would then oppose it. He must also reserve another case for his opposition; and this would be, if the evils of which he took cognizance should appear not to have been well founded. He had written to his constituents to be made acquainted with this

circumstance, and he must be guided by them on
the subject.

Mr. Martin was surprised how any person could
give an opposition to such a bill. Whatever were
the merits of the great question, all would allow
that, if human beings were to be transported across
the ocean, they should be carried over it with as
little suffering as possible to themselves.

Mr. Hamilton deprecated the subdivision of this
great and important question, which the house
had reserved for another session. Every endeavor
to meddle with one part of it, before the whole
of it could be taken into consideration, looked
rather as if it came from an enemy than from a
friend. He was fearful that such a bill as this
would sanction a traffic, which should never be
viewed but in a hostile light, or as repugnant to
the feelings of our nature, and to the voice of our
religion.

Lord Frederick Campbell was convinced that
the postponing of all consideration of the subject
till the next session was a wise measure. He
was sure that neither the house nor the public were
in a temper sufficiently cool to discuss it properly.
There was a general warmth of feeling, or an
enthusiasm about it, which ran away with the
understandings of men, and disqualified them from
judging soberly concerning it. He wished, therefore, that the present motion might be deferred.

Mr. William Smith said, that if the motion of
the honorable baronet had trespassed upon the
great question reserved for consideration, he would

have opposed it himself; but he conceived the subject, which it comprehended, might with propriety be separately considered; and if it were likely that a hundred, but much more a thousand, lives would be saved by this bill, it was the duty of that house to adopt it without delay.

The chancellor of the exchequer, though he meant still to conceal his opinion as to the general merits of the question, could not be silent here. He was of opinion that he could very consistently give this motion his support. There was a possibility (and a bare possibility was a sufficient ground with him) that in consequence of the resolution lately come to by the house, and the temper then manifested in it, those persons who were concerned in the Slave-trade might put the natives of Africa in a worse situation, during their transportation to the colonies, even than they were in before, by cramming additional numbers on board their vessels, in order to convey as many as possible to the West Indies before Parliament ultimately decided on the subject. The possibility, therefore, that such a consequence might grow out of their late resolution during the intervening months between the end of the present and the commencement of the next session, was a good and sufficient parliamentary ground for them to provide immediate means to prevent the existence of such an evil. He considered this as an act of indispensable duty, and on that ground the bill should have his support.

Soon after this the question was put, and leave was given for the introduction of the bill.

An account of these proceedings of the house having been sent to the merchants of Liverpool, they held a meeting, and came to resolutions on the subject. They determined to oppose the bill in every stage in which it should be brought forward, and what was extraordinary, even the principle of it. Accordingly, between the twenty-first of May and the second of June, on which latter day the bill, having been previously read a second time, was to be committed, petitions from interested persons had been brought against it, and consent had been obtained, that both counsel and evidence should be heard.

The order of the day having been read on the second of June for the house to resolve itself into a committee of the whole house, a discussion took place relative to the manner in which the business was to be conducted. This being over, the counsel began their observations; and, as soon as they had finished, evidence was called to the bar in behalf of the petitions which had been delivered.

From the second of June to the seventeenth the house continued to hear the evidence at intervals, but the members for Liverpool took every opportunity of occasioning delay. They had recourse twice to counting out the house; and at another time, though complaint had been made of their attempts to procrastinate, they opposed the resuming of their own evidence with the same view, and this merely for the frivolous reason, that, though

there was then a suitable opportunity, notice had
not been previously given. But in this proceeding
other members feeling indignant at their conduct,
they were overruled.

The witnesses brought by the Liverpool merchants against this humane bill were the same as
they had before sent for examination to the privy
council, namely, Mr. Norris, lieutenant Matthews,
and others. On the other side of the question it
was not deemed expedient to bring any. It was
soon perceived that it would be possible to refute
the former out of their own mouths, and to do this
seemed more eligible than to proceed in the other
way. Mr. Pitt, however, took care to send captain Parry, of the royal navy, to Liverpool, that he
might take the tonnage and internal dimensions
of several slave-vessels, which were then there,
supposing that these, when known, would enable
the house to detect any misrepresentations, which
the delegates from that town might be disposed
to make upon this subject.

It was the object of the witnesses, when examined, to prove two things : first, that regulations
were unnecessary, because the present mode of
the transportation was sufficiently convenient for
the objects of it, and was well adapted to preserve
their comfort and their health. They had sufficient room, sufficient air, and sufficient provisions.
When upon deck, they made merry and amused
themselves with dancing. As to the mortality, or
the loss of them by death in the course of their
passage, it was trifling. In short, the voyage

from Africa to the West Indies "was one of the
happiest periods of a negro's life."

Secondly, that if the merchants were hindered
from taking less than two full-sized, or three
smaller Africans, to a ton, then the restriction
would operate not as the regulation but as the
utter ruin of the trade. Hence the present bill,
under the specious mask of a temporary interference, sought nothing less than its abolition.

These assertions having been severally made,
by the former of which it was insinuated that the
African, unhappy in his own country, found in the
middle passage, under the care of the merchants,
little less than an Elysian retreat, it was now
proper to institute a severe inquiry into the truth
of them. Mr. Pitt, Sir Charles Middleton, Mr.
William Smith, and Mr. Beaufoy, took a conspicuous part on the occasion, but particularly the two
latter, to whom much praise was due for the constant attention they bestowed upon this subject.
Question after question was put by these to the witnesses; and from their own mouths they dragged
out, by means of a cross-examination as severe as
could be well instituted, the following melancholy
account:

Every slave, whatever his size might be, was
found to have only five feet and six inches in
length, and sixteen inches in breadth, to lie in.
The floor was covered with bodies stowed or
packed according to this allowance. But between
the floor and the deck or ceiling were often platforms or broad shelves in the midway, which were

covered with bodies also. The height from the floor to the ceiling, within which space the bodies on the floor and those on the platforms lay, seldom exceeded five feet eight inches, and in some cases it did not exceed four feet.

The men were chained two and two together by their hands and feet, and were chained also by means of ring-bolts, which were fastened to the deck. They were confined in this manner at least all the time they remained upon the coast, which was from six weeks to six months as it might happen.

Their allowance consisted of one pint of water a day to each person, and they were fed twice a day with yams and horse-beans.

After meals they jumped up in their irons for exercise. This was so necessary for their health, that they were whipped if they refused to do it. And this jumping had been termed dancing.

They were usually fifteen and sixteen hours below deck out of the twenty-four. In rainy weather they could not be brought up for two or three days together. If the ship was full, their situation was then distressing. They sometimes drew their breath with anxious and laborious efforts, and some died of suffocation.

With respect to their health in these voyages, the mortality, where the African constitution was the strongest, or on the windward coast, was only about five in a hundred. In thirty-five voyages, an account of which was produced, about six in a hundred was the average number lost. But this

loss was still greater at Calabar and Bonny, which
were the greatest markets for slaves. This loss,
too, did not include those who died, either while
the vessels were lying upon the coast, or after
their arrival in the West Indies, of the disorders
which they had contracted upon the voyage.
Three and four in a hundred had been known
to die in this latter case.

But besides these facts, which were forced out
of the witnesses by means of the cross-examination
which took place, they were detected in various
falsehoods.

They had asserted that the ships in this trade
were peculiarly constructed, or differently from
others, in order that they might carry a great
number of persons with convenience; whereas,
captain Parry asserted that out of the twenty-
six, which he had seen, ten only had been built
expressly for this employ.

They had stated the average height between
decks at about five feet and four inches. But
captain Parry showed, that out of the nine he
measured, the height in four of the smallest was
only four feet eight inches, and the average height
in all of them was but five feet two.

They had asserted that vessels under two hundred tons had no platforms. But by his account
the four just mentioned were of this tonnage,
and yet all of them had platforms either wholly
or in part.

On other points they were found both to contradict themselves and one another. They had

asserted, as before mentioned, that if they were restricted to less than two full-grown slaves to a ton, the trade would be ruined. But in examining into the particulars of nineteen vessels, which they produced themselves, five of them only had cargoes equal to the proportion which they stated to be necessary to the existence of the trade. The other fourteen carried a less number of slaves (and they might have taken more on board if they had pleased): so that the average number in the nineteen was but one man and four-fifths to a ton, or ten in a hundred below their lowest standard.* One again said, that no inconvenience arose in consequence of the narrow space allowed to each individual in these voyages. Another said, that smaller vessels were more healthy than larger, because, among other reason, they had a less proportion of slaves as to number on board.

They were found also guilty of a wilful concealment of such facts, as they knew, if communicated, would have invalidated their own testimony. I was instrumental in detecting them on one of these occasions myself. When Mr. Dalzell was examined, he was not wholly unknown to me. My Liverpool muster-rolls told me that he had lost fifteen seamen out of forty in his last voyage. This was a sufficient ground to go upon; for generally, where the mortality of the seamen has

* The falsehood of their statements in this respect was proved again afterwards by facts. For, after the regulation had taken place, they lost fewer slaves and made greater profits.

been great, it may be laid down that the mortality of the slaves has been considerable also. I waited patiently till his evidence was nearly closed, but he had then made no unfavorable statements to the house. I desired, therefore, that a question might be put to him, and in such a manner, that he might know that they, who put it, had got a clew to his secrets. He became immediately embarrassed. His voice faltered. He confessed with trembling, that he had lost a third of his sailors in his last voyage. Pressed hard immediately by other questions, he then acknowledged that he had lost one hundred and twenty or a third of his slaves also. But would he say that these were all he had lost in that voyage? No: twelve others had perished by an accident, for they were drowned. But were no others lost besides the one hundred and twenty and the twelve? None, he said, upon the voyage, but between twenty and thirty, before he left the coast. Thus this champion of the merchants, this advocate for the health and happiness of the slaves in the middle passage, lost nearly a hundred and sixty of the unhappy persons committed to his superior care, in a single voyage!

The evidence, on which I have now commented, having been delivered, the counsel summed up on the seventeenth of June, when the committee proceeded to fill up the blanks in the bill. Mr. Pitt moved that the operation of it be retrospective, and that it commence from the tenth instant. This was violently opposed by Lord Penrhyn, Mr.

Gascoyne, and Mr. Brickdale, but was at length acceded to.

Sir William Dolben then proposed to apportion five men to every three tons in every ship under one hundred and fifty tons burthen, which had the space of five feet between the decks, and three men to two tons in every vessel beyond one hundred and fifty tons burthen, which had equal accommodation in point of height between the decks. This occasioned a very warm dispute, which was not settled for some time, and which gave rise to some beautiful and interesting speeches on the subject.

Mr. William Smith pointed out in the clearest manner many of the contradictions, which I have just stated in commenting upon the evidence. Indeed he had been a principal means of detecting them. He proved how little worthy of belief the witnesses had shown themselves, and how necessary they had made the present bill by their own confession. The worthy baronet, indeed, had been too indulgent to the merchants, in the proportion he had fixed of the number of persons to be carried to the tonnage of their vessels. He then took a feeling view of what would be the wretched state of the poor Africans on board, even if the bill passed as it now stood; and conjured the house, if they would not allow them more room, at least not to infringe upon that, which had been proposed.

Lord Belgrave (now Grosvenor) animadverted with great ability upon the cruelties of the trade,

which he said had been fully proved at the bar.
He took notice of the extraordinary opposition
which had been made to the bill then before them,
and which he believed every gentleman, who had
a proper feeling of humanity, would condemn. If
the present mode of carrying on the trade received
the countenance of that house, the poor unfortunate African would have occasion doubly to curse
his fate. He would not only curse the womb that
brought him fourth, but the British nation also,
whose diabolical avarice had made his cup of
misery still more bitter. He hoped that the members for Liverpool would urge no further opposition
to the bill, but that they would join with the
house in an effort to enlarge the empire of humanity ; and that, while they were stretching out
the strong arm of justice to punish the degraders
of British honor and humanity in the East, they
would with equal spirit, exert their powers to dis-
pense the blessings of their protection to those
unhappy Africans, who were to serve them in
the West.

   Mr. Beaufoy entered minutely into an examination of the information, which had been given by
the witnesses, and which afforded unanswerable
arguments for the passing of the bill. He showed
the narrow space, which they themselves had been
made to allow for the package of a human body,
and the ingenious measures they were obliged to
resort to for stowing this living cargo within the
limits of the ship. He adverted next to the case
of Mr. Dalzell ; and showed how one dismal fact

after another, each making against their own
testimony, was extorted from him. He then went
to the trifling mortality said to be experienced in
these voyages, upon which subject he spoke in the
following words: "Though the witnesses are some
of them interested in the trade, and all of them
parties against the bill, their confession is, that of
the negroes of the windward coast, who are men
of the strongest constitution which Africa affords,
no less on an average than five in each hundred
perish in the voyage; a voyage, it must be remembered, but of six weeks. In a twelvemonth, then,
what must be the proportion of the dead? No
less than forty-three in a hundred, which is seventeen times the usual rate of mortality; for all the
estimates of life suppose no more than a fortieth
of the people, or two and a half in the hundred,
to die within the space of a year. Such then is
the comparison. In the ordinary course of nature
the number of persons (including those in age and
infancy, the weakest periods of existence) who
perish in the space of a twelvemonth, is at the
rate of but two and a half in a hundred; but in
an African voyage, notwithstanding the old are
excluded and few infants admitted, so that those
who are shipped are in the firmest period of life,
the list of deaths presents an annual mortality
of forty-three in a hundred. It presents this mortality even in vessels from the windward coast of
Africa; but in those which sail to Bonny, Benin,
and the Calabars, from whence the greatest proportion of the slaves are brought, this mortality

is increased by a variety of causes, (of which the
greater length of the voyage is one), and is said
to be twice as large, which supposes that in every
hundred the deaths annually amount to no less
than eighty-six. Yet even the former compara-
tively low mortality, of which the counsel speaks
with so much satisfaction, as a proof of the kind
and compassionate treatment of the slaves, even
this indolent and lethargic destruction gives to
the march of death seventeen times its usual
speed. It is a destruction, which, if general but
for ten years, would depopulate the world, blast
the purposes of its creation, and extinguish the
human race."

After having gone with great ability through
the other branches of the subject, he concluded in
the following manner : "Thus I have considered
the various objections which had been stated to
the bill, and am ashamed to reflect that it could
be necessary to speak so long in defence of such
a cause : for what, after all, is asked by the proposed regulations ? On the part of the Africans,
the whole of their purport is, that they, whom
you allow to be robbed of all things but life, may
not unnecessarily and wantonly be deprived of life
also. To the honor, to the wisdom, to the feelings of the house I now make my appeal, perfectly
confident that you will not tolerate, as senators, a
traffic, which, as men, you shudder to contemplate,
and that you will not take upon yourselves, the
responsibility of this waste of existence. To the
memory of former Parliaments the horrors of this

traffic will be an eternal reproach; yet former Parliaments have not known, as you in the clearest evidence now know, the dreadful nature of this trade. Should you reject this bill, no exertions of yours to rescue from oppression the suffering inhabitants of your Eastern empire; no records of the prosperous state to which, after a long and unsuccessful war, you have restored your native land; no proofs, however splendid, that, under your guidance, Great Britain has recovered her rank, and is again the arbitress of nations, will save your names from the stigma of everlasting dishonor. The broad mantle of this one infamy will cover with substantial blackness the radiance of your glory, and change to feelings of abhorrence the present admiration of the world. But pardon the supposition of so impossible an event. I believe that justice and mercy may be considered as the attributes of your character, and that you will not tarnish their lustre, on this occasion."

The chancellor of the exchequer rose next; and after having made some important observations on the evidence, (which took up much time), he declared himself most unequivocally in favor of the motion made by the honorable baronet. He was convinced that the regulation proposed would not tend to the abolition of the trade; but if it even went so far, he had no hesitation openly and boldly to declare, that if it could not be carried on in a manner different from that stated by the members for Liverpool, he would retract wha

he had said on a former day against going into
the general question; and, waving every other
discussion than what had that day taken place, he
would give his vote for the utter annihilation of it
at once. It was a trade, which it was shocking to
humanity to hear detailed. If it were to be carried
on as proposed by the petitioners, it would, besides
its own intrinsic baseness, be contrary to every
humane and Christian principle, and to every
sentiment that ought to inspire the breast of man,
and would reflect the greatest dishonor on the
British senate and the British nation. He therefore hoped that the house, being now in possession of such information as never hitherto had
been brought before them, would in some measure
endeavor to extricate themselves from that guilt,
and from that remorse, which every one of them
ought to feel for having suffered such monstrous
cruelties to be practised upon an helpless and unoffending part of the human race.

Mr. Martin complimented Mr. Pitt in terms of
the warmest panegyric on his noble sentiments,
declaring that they reflected the greatest honor
upon him both as an Englishman and as a man.

Soon after this the house divided upon the motion of Sir William Dolben. Fifty-six appeared to
be in favor of it, and only five against it. The
latter consisted of the two members for Liverpool
and three other interested persons. This was the
first division which ever took place on this important subject. The other blanks were then filled
up, and the bill was passed without further delay.

The next day, or on the eighteenth of June, it was carried up to the House of Lords. The slave-merchants of London, Liverpool, and Bristol, immediately presented petitions against it, as they had done in the lower house. They prayed that counsel might open their case; and though they had been driven from the commons, on account of their evidence, with disgrace, they had the effrontery to ask that they might call witnesses here also.

Counsel and evidence having been respectively heard, the bill was ordered to be committed the next day. The lords attended according to summons. But on a motion by Dr. Warren, the bishop of Bangor, who stated that the lord chancellor Thurlow was much indisposed, and that he wished to be present when the question was discussed, the committee was postponed.

It was generally thought that the reason for this postponement, and particularly as it was recommended by a prelate, was, that the chancellor might have an opportunity of forwarding this humane bill. But it was found to be quite otherwise. It appeared that the motive was, that he might give to it, by his official appearance as the chief servant of the crown in that house, all the opposition in his power. For when the day arrived, which had been appointed for the discussion, and when the lords Bathurst and Hawkesbury, (now Liverpool), had expressed their opinions, which were different, relative to the time when the bill should take place, he rose up, and

pronounced a bitter and vehement oration against
it. He said, among other things, that it was full
of inconsistency and nonsense from the beginning
to the end. The French had lately offered large
premiums for the encouragement of this trade.
They were a politic people, and the presumption
was, that we were doing politically wrong by
abandoning it. The bill ought not to have been
brought forward in this session. The introduction
of it was a direct violation of the faith of the other
house. It was unjust, when an assurance had been
given that the question should not be agitated till
next year, that this sudden fit of philanthropy
which was but a few days old, should be allowed
to disturb the public mind, and to become the occasion of bringing men to the metropolis with tears
in their eyes and horror in their countenances, to
deprecate the ruin of their property, which they
had embarked on the faith of Parliament.

The extraordinary part, which the lord chancellor Thurlow took upon this occasion, was ascribed
at the time by many, who moved in the higher
circles, to a shyness or misunderstanding, which
had taken place between him and Mr. Pitt on
other matters; when, believing this bill to have
been a favorite measure with the latter, he determined to oppose it. But, whatever were his motives, (and let us hope that he could never have
been actuated by so malignant a spirit as that
of sacrificing the happiness of forty thousand persons for the next year to spite the gratification of
an individual), his opposition had a mischievous

effect, on account of the high situation in which he stood. For he not only influenced some of the lords themselves, but, by taking the cause of the slave-merchants so conspicuously under his wing, he gave them boldness to look up again under the stigma of their iniquitous calling, and courage even to resume vigorous operations after their disgraceful defeat. Hence arose those obstacles, which will be found to have been thrown in the way of the passing of the bill from this period.

Among the lords, who are to be particularly noticed as having taken the same side as the lord chancellor in this debate, were the duke of Chandos and the earl of Sandwich. The former foresaw nothing but insurrections of the slaves in our islands, and the massacre of their masters there, in consequence of the agitation of this question. The latter expected nothing less than the ruin of our marine. He begged the house to consider how, by doing that which might bring about the abolition of this traffic, they might lessen the number of British sailors; how, by throwing it into the hands of France, they might increase those of a rival nation; and how, in consequence, the flag of the latter might ride triumphant on the ocean. The Slave-trade was undoubtedly a nursery for our seamen. All objections against it in this respect were ill-founded. It was as healthy as the Newfoundland and many other trades.

The debate having closed, during which nothing more was done than filling up the blanks with the

time when the bill was to begin to operate, the
committee was adjourned. But the bill after this
dragged on so heavily, that it would be tedious to
detail the proceedings upon it from day to day.
I shall, therefore, satisfy myself with the following
observations concerning them. The committee
sat not less than five different times, which con-
sumed the space of eight days, before a final
decision took place. During this time, so much
was it an object to throw in obstacles which might
occupy the little remaining time of the session,
that other petitions were presented against the bill,
and leave was asked, on new pretences contained in
these, that counsel might be heard again. Letters
also were read from Jamaica, about the mutinous
disposition of the slaves there, in consequence of
the stir which had been made about the abolition,
and also from merchants in France, by which
large offers were made to the British merchants
to furnish them with slaves. Several regulations
also were proposed in this interval, some of which
were negatived by majorities of only one or two
voices. Of the regulations, which were carried,
the most remarkable were those proposed by lord
Hawkesbury (now Liverpool); namely, that no
insurance should be made on the slaves except
against accidents by fire and water; that persons
should not be appointed as officers of vessels transporting them, who had not been a certain number
of such voyages before; that a regular surgeon
only should be capable of being employed in them;
and that both the captain and surgeon should have

bounties, if in the course of the transportation they
had lost only two in a hundred slaves. The duke
of Chandos again, and lord Sydney, were the most
conspicuous among the opposers of this humane
bill ; and the duke of Richmond, the marquis
Townshend, the earl of Carlisle, the bishop of
London, and earl Stanhope, among the most strenuous supporters of it.   At length it passed, by a
majority of nineteen to eleven votes.

On the fourth of July, when the bill had been
returned to the commons, it was moved that the
amendments made in it by the lords should be
read ; but as it had become a money-bill in consequence of the bounties to be granted, and as new
regulations were to be incorporated in it, it was
thought proper that it should be wholly done
away.   Accordingly Sir William Dolben moved,
that the further consideration of it should be put
off till that day three months. This having been
agreed upon, he then moved for leave to bring
in a new bill. This was accordingly introduced,
and an additional clause was inserted in it, relative to bounties by Mr. Pitt.   But on the second
reading, that no obstacle might be omitted which
could legally be thrown in the way of its progress,
petitions were presented against it both by the
Liverpool merchants and the agent for the island
of Jamaica, under the pretence that it was a new
bill.   Their petitions, however, were rejected, and
it was committed, and passed through its regular
stages and sent up to the lords.

On its arrival there on the fifth of July, petitions

from London and Liverpool still followed it. The prayer of these was against the general tendency of it, but it was solicited also that counsel might be heard in a particular case. The solicitation was complied with ; after which the bill was read a second time, and ordered to be committed.

On the seventh, when it was taken next into consideration, two other petitions were presented against it. But here so many objections were made to the clauses of it as they then stood, and such new matter suggested, that the duke of Richmond, who was a strenuous supporter of it, thought it best to move that the committee, then sitting, should be deferred till that day sevennight, in order to give time for another more perfect to originate in the lower house.

This motion having been acceded to, Sir William Dolben introduced a new one for the third time into the commons. This included the suggestions which had been made in the lords. It included also a regulation, on the motion of Mr. Sheridan, that no surgeon should be employed as such in the slave vessels, except he had a testimonial that he had passed a proper examination at Surgeon's Hall. The amendments were all then agreed to, and the bill was passed through its several stages.

On the tenth of July, being now fully amended, it came for a third time before the lords ; but it was no sooner brought forward than it met with the same opposition as it had experienced before. Two new petitions appeared against it, one from

a certain class of persons in Liverpool, and another
from Miles Peter Andrews, esquire, stating that,
if it passed into a law, it would injure the sale of
his gunpowder, and that he had rendered great
services to the government during the last war by
his provision of that article. But here the lord
chancellor Thurlow reserved himself for an effort,
which, by occasioning only a day's delay, would
in that particular period of the session have totally
prevented the passing of the bill. He suggested
certain amendments for consideration and discussion, which, if they had been agreed upon, must
have been carried again to the lower house and
sanctioned there before the bill could have been
complete. But it appeared afterwards, that there
would have been no time for the latter proceeding.
Earl Stanhope, therefore, pressed this circumstance
peculiarly upon the lords who were present. He
observed, that the king was to dismiss the Parliament next day, and therefore they must adopt
the bill as it stood, or reject it altogether. There
was no alternative, and no time was to be lost.
Accordingly he moved for an immediate division
on the first of the amendments proposed by lord
Thurlow. This having taken place, it was negatived. The other amendments shared the same
fate; and thus, at length, passed through the
upper house, as through an ordeal as it were of
fire, the first bill that ever put fetters upon that
barbarous and destructive monster, the Slave-
trade.

The next day, or on Friday, July the eleventh,

the king gave his assent to it, and, as lord Stanhope had previously asserted in the house of lords,
concluded the session.

While the legislature was occupied in the consideration of this bill, the lords of the council continued their examinations, that they might collect
as much light as possible previously to the general
agitation of the question in the next session of Parliament. Among others I underwent an examination. I gave my testimony first relative to many
of the natural productions of Africa, of which I
produced the specimens. These were such as I
had collected in the course of my journey to Bristol and Liverpool, and elsewhere. I explained,
secondly, the loss and usage of seamen in the
Slave-trade. To substantiate certain points, which
belonged to this branch of the subject, I left
several depositions and articles of agreement for
the examination of the council. With respect to
others, as it would take a long time to give all the
data upon which calculations had been made and
the manner of making them, I was desired to
draw up a statement of particulars, and to send it
to the council at a future time. I left also depositions with them relative to certain instances of the
mode of procuring and treating slaves.

The committee also for effecting the abolition
of the Slave-trade continued their attention, during this period, towards the promotion of the different objects, which came within the range of
the institution.

They added the reverend Dr. Coombe, in consequence of the great increase of their business, to the list of. their members.

They voted thanks to Mr. Hughes, vicar of Ware in Hertfordshire, for his excellent Answer to Harris's Scriptural Researches on the Licitness of the Slave-trade, and they enrolled him among their honorary and corresponding members. Also thanks to William Roscoe, esquire, for his Answer to the same. Mr. Roscoe had not affixed his name to this pamphlet any more than to his poem of the Wrongs of Africa. But he made himself known to the committee as the author of both. Also thanks to William Smith and Henry Beaufoy, esquires, for having so successfully exposed the evidence offered by the slave-merchants against the bill of Sir William Dolben, and for having drawn out of it so many facts, all making for their great object the abolition of the Slave-trade.

As the great question was to be discussed in the approaching sessions, it was moved in the committee to consider of the propriety of sending persons to Africa and the West Indies, who should obtain information relative to the different branches of the system as they existed in each of these countries, in order that they might be able to give their testimony, from their own experience, before one or both of the houses of Parliament, as it might be judged proper. This proposition was discussed at two or three several meetings. It was however finally rejected, and principally on the following grounds: First, It was obvious, that persons sent out upon such an errand would be exposed to such dangers from various causes, that it was not improbable that both they and their testimony might be lost. Secondly, such persons would be obliged to have recourse to falsehoods, that is, to conceal or misrepresent the object of their destination, that they might get their intelligence with safety; which falsehoods the committee could not countenance. To which it was added, that few persons would go to these places, except they were handsomely rewarded for their trouble; but this reward would lessen the value of their evidence, as it would afford a handle to the planters and slave-merchants to say that they had been bribed.

Another circumstance, which came before the committee, was the following: Many arguments were afloat at this time relative to the great impolicy of abolishing the Slave-trade, the principal of which was, that, if the English abandoned it, other foreign nations would take it up; and thus, while they gave up certain national profits themselves, the great cause of humanity would not be benefited, nor would any moral good be done by the measure. Now there was a presumption that, by means of the society instituted in Paris, the French nation might be awakened to this great subject, and that the French government might in consequence, as well as upon other considerations, be induced to favor the general feeling upon this occasion. But there was no reason to conclude, either that any other maritime people, who had been engaged in the Slave-trade, would relinquish

it, or that any other, who had not yet been engaged in it, would not begin it when our countrymen should give it up. The consideration of
these circumstances occupied the attention of the
committee; and as Dr. Spaarman, who was said
to have been examined by the privy council, was
returning home, it was thought advisable to consider whether it would not be proper for the committee to select certain of their own books on the
subject of the Slave-trade, and send them by him,
accompanied by a letter, to the king of Sweden,
in which they should entreat his consideration
of this powerful argument which now stood in the
way of the cause of humanity, with a view that,
as one of the princes of Europe, he might contribute to obviate it, by preventing his own subjects, in case of the dereliction of this commerce
by ourselves, from embarking in it. The matter
having been fully considered, it was resolved that
the proposed measure would be proper, and it was
accordingly adopted. By a letter received afterwards from Dr. Spaarman, it appeared that both
the letter and the books had been delivered, and
received graciously; and that he was authorized
to say, that unfortunately, in consequence of those
hereditary possessions which had devolved upon
his majesty, he was obliged to confess that he
was the sovereign of an island, which had been
principally peopled by African slaves, but that he
had been frequently mindful of their hard case.
With respect to the Slave-trade, he never heard
of an instance, in which the merchants of his

own native realm had embarked in it; and as
they had hitherto preserved their character pure
in this respect, he would do all he could that it
should not be sullied in the eyes of the generous
English nation, by taking up, in the case which
had been pointed out to him, such an odious
concern.

By this time I had finished my Essay on the Impolicy of the Slave-trade, which I composed from
materials collected chiefly during my journey to
Bristol, Liverpool, and Lancaster. These materials I had admitted with great caution and cir-
cumspection; indeed I admitted none, for which
I could not bring official and other authentic documents, or living evidences if necessary, whose
testimony could not reasonably be denied; and,
when I gave them to the world, I did it under the
impression that I ought to give them as scrupu-
lously as if I were to be called upon to substantiate them upon oath. It was of peculiar moment
that this book should make its appearance at this
time. First, because it would give the lords of the
council, who were then sitting, an opportunity of
seeing many important facts, and of inquiring
into their authenticity; and it might suggest to
them also some new points, or such as had not
fallen within the limits of the arrangement they
had agreed upon for their examinations on this
subject; and, secondly, because, as the members
of the House of Commons were to take the question into consideration early in the next sessions,
it would give them also new light and information

upon it before this period.   Accordingly the committee ordered two thousand copies of it to be struck off, for these and other objects; and though the contents of it were most diligently sifted by the different opponents of the cause, they never even made an attempt to answer it.   It continued, on the other hand, during the inquiry of the legislature, to afford the basis or grounds upon which to examine evidences on the political part of the subject; and evidences thus examined continued in their turn to establish it.

. Among the other books ordered to be printed by the committee within the period now under our consideration, were a new edition of two thousand of the Dean of Middleham's Letter, and another of three thousand of Falconbridge's Account of the Slave-trade.

The committee continued to keep up, during the same period, a communication with many of their old correspondents, whose names have been already mentioned.   But they received also letters from others, who had not hitherto addressed them; namely, from Ellington Wright of Erith, Dr. Franklin of Philadelphia, Eustace Kentish, esquire, high sheriff for the county of Huntingdon, Governor Bouchier, the reverend Charles Symmons of Haverfordwest; and from John York and William Downes, esquires, high sheriffs for the counties of York and Hereford.

A letter also was read in this interval from Mr. Evans, a dissenting clergyman, of Bristol, stating that the elders of several Baptist churches, forming the western Baptist association, who had met at Portsmouth Common, had resolved to recommend it to the ministers and members of the same, to unite with the committee in the promotion of the great object of their institution.

Another from Mr. Andrew Irvin, of the island of Grenada, in which he confirmed the wretched situation of many of the slaves there, and in which he gave the outlines of a plan for bettering their condition, as well as that of those in the other islands.

Another from I. L. Wyne, esquire, of Jamaica. In this he gave an afflicting account of the suffering and unprotected state of the slaves there, which it was high time to rectify. He congratulated the committee on their institution, which he thought would tend to promote so desirable an end; but desired them not to stop short of the total abolition of the Slave-trade, as no other measure would prove effectual against the evils of which he complained. This trade, he said, was utterly unnecessary, as his own plantation, on which his slaves had increased rapidly by population, and others which he knew to be similarly circumstanced, would abundantly testify. He concluded by promising to give the committee such information from time to time as might be useful on this important subject.

The sessions of parliament having closed, the committee thought it right to make a report to the public, in which they gave an account of the great progress of their cause since the last, of the state in which they then were, and of the unjustifiable conduct of their opponents, who industriously misrepresented their views, and particularly by attributing to them the design of abolishing slavery; and they concluded by exhorting their friends not to relax their endeavors, on account of favorable appearances, but to persevere, as if nothing had been done, under the pleasing hope of an honorable triumph.

And now having given the substance of the labors of the committee from its formation to the present time, I cannot conclude this chapter without giving to the worthy members of it that tribute of affectionate and grateful praise, which is due to them for their exertions in having forwarded the great cause which was intrusted to their care. And this I can do with more propriety, because, having been so frequently absent from them when they were engaged in the pursuit of this their duty, I cannot be liable to the suspicion, that in bestowing commendation upon them I am bestowing it upon myself. From about the end of May, 1787, to the middle of July, 1788, they had held no less than fifty-one committees. These generally occupied them from about six in the evening till about eleven at night. In the intervals between the committees they were often occupied, having each of them some object committed to his charge. It is remarkable, too, that though they were all except one engaged in business or trade, and though they had the same calls as other men for innocent recreation, and the same interruptions of their health, there were individuals, who were not absent more than five or six times within this period. In the course of the thirteen months, during which they had exercised this public trust, they had printed, and afterwards distributed, not at random, but judiciously, and through respectable channels, (besides twenty-six thousand five hundred and twenty-six reports, accounts of debates in Parliament, and other small papers,) no less than fifty-one thousand four hundred and thirty-two pamphlets, or books.

Nor was the effect produced within this short period otherwise than commensurate with the efforts used. In May, 1787, the only public notice taken of this great cause was by this committee of twelve individuals, of whom all were little known to the world except Mr. Granville Sharp. But in July, 1788, it had attracted the notice of several distinguished individuals in France and Germany, and in our own country it had come within the notice of the government, and a branch of it had undergone a parliamentary discussion and restraint. It had arrested also the attention of the nation, and it had produced a kind of holy flame, or enthusiasm, and this to a degree and to an extent never before witnessed. Of the purity of this flame no better proof can be offered, than that even bishops deigned to address an obscure committee, consisting principally of Quakers, and that churchmen and dissenters forgot their difference of religious opinions, and joined their hands, all over the kingdom, in its support.

CHAPTER VIII.

CONTINUATION FROM JUNE, 1788, TO JULY, 1789.—AUTHOR TRAVELS TO COLLECT FURTHER EVIDENCE—GREAT DIFFICULTIES IN OBTAINING IT—FORMS COMMITTEES ON HIS TOUR.—PRIVY COUNCIL RESUME THE EXAMINATIONS—INSPECT CABINET OF AFRICAN PRODUCTIONS—OBLIGED TO LEAVE MANY OF THE WITNESSES IN BEHALF OF THE ABOLITION UNEXAMINED—PREPARE THEIR REPORT.—LABORS OF THE COMMITTEE IN THE INTERIM.—PROCEEDINGS OF THE PLANTERS AND OTHERS.—REPORT LAID ON THE TABLE OF THE HOUSE OF COMMONS—INTRODUCTION OF THE QUESTION, AND DEBATE THERE—TWELVE PROPOSITIONS DEDUCED FROM THE REPORT AND RESERVED FOR FUTURE DISCUSSION—DAY OF DISCUSSION ARRIVES—OPPONENTS REFUSE TO ARGUE FROM THE REPORT—REQUIRE NEW EVIDENCE—THIS GRANTED AND INTRODUCED—FURTHER CONSIDERATION OF THE SUBJECT DEFERRED TO THE NEXT SESSION.—RENEWAL OF SIR WILLIAM DOLBEN'S BILL.—DEATH AND CHARACTER OF RAMSAY.

MATTERS had now become serious. The gauntlet had been thrown down and accepted. The combatants had taken their stations, and the contest was to be renewed, which was to be decided soon on the great theatre of the nation. The committee by the very act of their institution had pronounced the Slave-trade to be criminal. They, on the other hand, who were concerned in it, had denied the charge. It became the one to prove, and the other to refute it, or to fall in the ensuing session.

The committee, in this perilous situation, were anxious to find out such other persons, as might become proper evidences before the privy council. They had hitherto sent there only nine or ten, and they had then only another whom they could count upon for this purpose, in their view. The proposal of sending persons to Africa, and the West Indies, who might come back and report what they had witnessed, had been already negatived. The question then was, what they were to do. Upon this they deliberated, and the result was an application to me to undertake a journey to different parts of the kingdom for this purpose.

When this determination was made I was at Teston, writing a long letter to the privy council on the ill-usage and mortality of the seamen employed in the Slave-trade, which it had been previously agreed should be received as evidence there. I thought it proper, however, before I took my departure, to form a system of questions upon the general subject. These I divided into six tables. The first related to the productions of Africa, and the disposition and manners of the natives. The second, to the methods of reducing them to slavery. The third, to the manner of bringing them to the ships, their value, the medium of exchange, and other circumstances. The fourth, to their transportation. The fifth, to their treatment in the colonies. The sixth, to the seamen employed in the trade. These tables contained together one hundred and forty-five questions. My idea was that they should be printed on a small sheet of paper, which should be folded up in seven or eight leaves, of the length and breadth of a small almanac, and then be sent in franks to our different correspondents. These, when they had them, might examine persons capable of giving evidence, who might live in their neighborhoods or fall in their way, and return us their examinations by letter.

The committee having approved and printed the tables of questions, I began my tour. I had selected the southern counties from Kent to Cornwall for it. I had done this, because these included the great stations of the ships of war in ordinary; and as these were all under the superintendence of Sir Charles Middleton, as comptroller of the navy, I could get an introduction to those on board them. Secondly, because seafaring people, when they retire from a marine life, usually settle in some town or village upon the coast.

Of this tour I shall not give the reader any very particular account. I shall mention only those things which are most worthy of his notice in it. At Poole in Dorsetshire I laid the foundation of a committee, to act in harmony with that of London for the promotion of the cause. Moses Neave, of the respectable society of the Quakers, was the chairman; Thomas Bell, the secretary, and Ellis B. Metford and the reverend Mr. Davis and others the committee. This was the third committee which had been instituted in the country for this purpose. That at Bristol, under Mr. Joseph Harford as chairman, and Mr. Lunell as secretary, had been the first. And that at Manchester, under Mr. Thomas Walker as chairman, and Mr. Samuel Jackson as secretary, had been the second.

.. As Poole was a great·place for carrying on the trade to Newfoundland, I determined to examine the assertion of the earl of Sandwich in the House of Lords, when he said, in the debate on Sir William Dolben's bill, that the Slave-trade was not more fatal to seamen than the Newfoundland and some others. This assertion I knew at the time to be erroneous, as far as my own researches had been concerned ; for out of twenty-four vessels, . which had sailed out of the port of Bristol in that employ, only two sailors were upon the dead list. In sixty vessels from Poole, I found but four lost. At Dartmouth, where I went afterwards on purpose, I found almost a similar result. On conversing, however, with governor Holdsworth, I learnt that the year 1786 had been more fatal than any other in this trade. I learnt that in consequence of extraordinary storms and hurricanes, no less than five sailors had died, and twenty-one had been drowned in eighty-three vessels from that port. Upon this statement I determined to look into the muster-rolls of the trade there for two or three years together. I began by accident. with the year 1769, and I went on to the end of 1772. About eighty vessels on an average had sailed thence in each of these years. Taking the loss in these years, and compounding it with that in the fatal year, three sailors had been lost, but taking it in these four years by themselves, only two had been lost, in twenty-four vessels so employed. On a comparison with the Slave-trade, the result would be, that two vessels to Africa would destroy more seamen than eighty-three sailing to Newfoundland.   There was this difference also to be noted, that the loss in the one trade was generally by the weather or by accident, but in the other by cruel treatment or disease; and that they, who went out in a declining state of health in the one, came home generally recovered, whereas they, who went out robust in the other, came home in a shattered condition.

At Plymouth I laid the foundation of another committee.   The late William Cookworthy, the late John Prideaux, and James Fox, all of the society of the Quakers, and Mr. George Leach, Samuel Northcote, and John Saunders, had a principal share in forming it.   Sir William Ellford was chosen chairman.

From Plymouth I journeyed on to Falmouth, and from thence to Exeter, where having meetings with the late Mr. Samuel Milford, the late Mr. George Manning, the reverend James Manning, Thomas Sparkes, and others, a desire became manifest among them of establishing a committee there.   This was afterwards effected; and Mr. Milford, who, at a general meeting of the inhabitants of Exeter, on the tenth of June, on this great subject, had been called by those present to the chair, was appointed the chairman of it.

With respect to evidence, which was the great object of this tour, I found myself often very unpleasantly situated in collecting it. · I heard of many persons capable of giving it to our advantage, to whom I could get no introduction.   I had to go after these many miles out of my established route. Not knowing me, they received me coldly, and even suspiciously ; while I fell in with others, who, considering themselves, on account of their concerns and connexions, as our opponents, treated me in an uncivil manner.

But the difficulties and disappointments in other respects, which I experienced in this tour, even where I had an introduction, and where the parties were not interested in the continuance of the Slave-trade, were greater than people in general would have imagined. One would have thought, considering the great enthusiasm of the nation on this important subject, that they, who could have given satisfactory information upon it, would have rejoiced to do it. But I found it otherwise, and this frequently to my sorrow. There was an aversion in persons to appear before such a tribunal as they conceived the privy council to be. With men of shy or timid character this operated as an insuperable barrier in their way. But it operated more or less upon all. It was surprising to see what little circumstances affected many. When I took out my pen and ink to put down the information, which a person was giving me, he became evidently embarrassed and frightened. He began to excuse himself from staying, by alleging that he had nothing more to communicate, and he took himself away as quickly as he could with decency. The sight of the pen and ink had lost me so many good evidences, that I was obliged wholly to abandon the use of them, and to betake myself to other

means. I was obliged for the future to commit
my tables of questions to memory, and endeavor
by practice to put down, after the examination of
a person, such answers as he had given me to
each of them.

Others went off because it happened that immediately on my interview, I acquainted them with
the nature of my errand, and solicited their attendance in London. Conceiving that I had no right
to ask them such a favor, or terrified at the ab-
ruptness and apparent awfulness of my request,
some of them gave me an immediate denial,
which they would never afterwards retract. I began to perceive in time that it was only by the
most delicate management that I could get forward on these occasions. I resolved therefore for
the future, except in particular cases, that, when
I should be introduced to persons who had a competent knowledge of this trade, I would talk with
them upon it as upon any ordinary subject, and
then leave them without saying any thing about
their becoming evidences. I would take care,
however, to commit all their conversation to writing, when it was over, and I would then try to
find out that person among their relations or
friends, who could apply to them for this purpose
with the least hazard of a refusal.

There were others also, who, though they were
not so much impressed by the considerations mentioned, yet objected to give their public testimony.
Those, whose livelihood, or promotion, or expectations, were dependant upon the government of
14*

the country, were generally backward upon these occasions. Though they thought they discovered in the parliamentary conduct of Mr. Pitt, a bias in favor of the cause, they knew to a certainty that the lord chancellor Thurlow was against it. They conceived, therefore, that the administration was at least divided upon the question, and they were fearful of being called upon least they should give offence, and thus injure their prospects in life. This objection was very prevalent in that part of the kingdom which I had selected for my tour.

The reader can hardly conceive how my mind was agitated and distressed on these different accounts. To have travelled more than two months, to have seen many who could have materially served our cause, and to have lost most of them, was very trying. And though it is true that I applied a remedy, I was not driven to the adoption of it till I had performed more than half my tour. Suffice it to say, that after having travelled upwards of sixteen hundred miles backwards and forwards, and having conversed with forty-seven persons, who were capable of promoting the cause by their evidence, I could only prevail upon nine, by all the interest I could make, to be examined.

On my return to London, whither I had been called up by the committee to take upon me the superintendence of the evidence, which the privy council was now ready again to hear, I found my brother: he was then a young officer in the navy;

and as I knew he felt as warmly as I did in this great cause, I prevailed upon him to go to Havre de Grace, the great slave-port in France, where he might make his observations for two or three months, and then report what he had seen and heard; so that we might have some one to counteract any false statement of things which might be made relative to the subject in that quarter.

At length the examinations were resumed, and with them the contest, in which our own reputation and the fate of our cause were involved. The committee for the abolition had discovered one or two willing evidences during my absence, and Mr. Wilberforce, who was now recovered from his severe indisposition, had found one or two others. These added to my own, made a respectable body: but we had sent no more than four or five of these to the council when the king's illness unfortunately stopped our career. For nearly five weeks between the middle of November and January the examinations were interrupted or put off, so that at the latter period we began to fear that there would be scarcely time to hear the rest; for not only the privy council report was to be printed, but the contest itself was to be decided by the evidence contained in it, in the existing session.

The examinations, however, went on, but they went on only slowly, being still subject to interruption from the same unfortunate cause. Among others I offered my mite of information again. I wished the council to see more of my African

productions and manufactures, that they might
really know what Africa was capable of affording
instead of the Slave-trade, and that they might
make a proper estimate of the genius and talents
of the natives. The samples which I had collected had been obtained by great labor, and at
no inconsiderable expense : for whenever I had
notice that a vessel had arrived immediately from
that continent, I never hesitated to go, unless
under the most pressing engagement elsewhere,
even as far as Bristol, if I could pick up but a
single new article. The lords having consented,
I selected several things for their inspection out
of my box, of the contents of which the following account may not be unacceptable to the
reader.

The first division of the box consisted of woods
of about four inches square, all polished. Among
these were mahogany of five different sorts, tulip
wood, satin wood, camwood, barwood, fustic,
black and yellow ebony, palm tree, mangrove,
calabash, and date. There were seven woods of
which the native names were remembered ; three
of these, tumiah, samain, and jimlaké, were of
a yellow color ; acajou was of a beautiful deep
crimson ; bork and quellé were apparently fit for
cabinet work ; and benten was the wood of which
the natives made their canoes. Of the various
other woods the names had been forgotten, nor
were they known in England at all. One of them
was of a fine purple ; and from two others, upon
which the privy council had caused experiments

to be made, a strong yellow, a deep orange, and a flesh color were extracted.

The second division included ivory and musk; four species of pepper, the long, the black, the Cayenne, and the Malaguetta: three species of gum; namely, Senegal, copal, and ruber astringens; cinnamon, rice, tobacco, indigo, white and Nankin cotton, Guinea corn, and millet; three species of beans, of which two were used for food, and the other for dyeing orange; two species of tamarinds, one for food, and the other to give whiteness to the teeth; pulse, seeds, and fruits of various kinds, some of the latter of which Dr. Spaarman had pronounced, from a trial during his residence in Africa, to be peculiarly valuable as drugs.

The third division contained an African loom, and an African spindle with spun cotton round it; cloths of cotton of various kinds, made by the natives, some white, but others dyed by them of different colors, and others, in which they had interwoven European silk; cloths and bags made of grass, and fancifully colored; ornaments made of the same materials; ropes made from a species of aloes, and others, remarkably strong, from grass and straw; fine string made from the fibres of the roots of trees; soap of two kinds, one of which was formed from an earthy substance; pipe bowls made of clay, and of a brown red; one of these, which came from the village of Dakard, was beautifully ornamented by black devices burnt in, and was besides highly glazed; another, brought from

Galam, was made of earth, which was richly impregnated with little particles of gold; trinkets made by the natives from their own gold; knives and daggers made by them from our bar iron; and various other articles, such as bags, sandals, dagger cases, quivers, grisgris, all made of leather of their own manufacture, and dyed of various colors, and ingeniously sewed together.

The fourth division consisted of the thumb-screw, speculum oris, and chains and shackles of different kinds, collected at Liverpool. To these were added, iron neck collars, and other instruments of punishment and confinement, used in the West Indies, and collected at other places. The instrument, also, by which Charles Horseler was mentioned to have been killed, in the former volume, was to be seen among these.

We were now advanced far into February, when we were alarmed by the intelligence that the lords of the council were going to prepare their report. At this time we had sent but few persons to them to examine, in comparison with our opponents, and we had yet eighteen to introduce: for answers had come into my tables of questions from several places, and persons had been pointed out to us by our correspondents, who had increased our list of evidences to this number. I wrote therefore to them, at the desire of the committee for the abolition, and gave them the names of the eighteen, and requested that all of them might be examined. I requested also, that they would order, for their own inspection, certain

muster-rolls of vessels from Poole and Dartmouth,
that they might be convinced that the objection
which the Earl of Sandwich had made in the
House of Lords, against the abolition of the Slave-
trade, had no solid foundation.   In reply to my
first request they informed me, that it was impossible, in the advanced state of the session (it being
then the middle of March), that the examinations
of so many could be taken ; but I was at liberty,
in conjunction with the bishop of London, to select
eight for this purpose.   This occasioned me to
address them again ; and I then found, to my
surprise and sorrow, that even this last number
was to be diminished ; for I was informed in
writing, " that the bishop of London having laid
my last letter before their lordships, they had
agreed to meet on the Saturday next, and on the
Tuesday following, for the purpose of receiving
the evidence of some of the gentlemen named in
it.   And it was their lordships' desire, that I would
give notice to any three of them (whose information I might consider as the most material), of the
above determination, that they might attend the
committee accordingly."

This answer, considering the difficulties we had
found in collecting a body of evidence, and the
critical situation in which we then were, was
peculiarly distressing ; but we had no remedy
left us, nor could we reasonably complain.   Three
therefore were selected, and they were sent to deliver their testimony on their arrival in town.

But before the last of these had left the council

room, who should come up to me but Mr. Arnold!
He had but lately arrived at Bristol from Africa:
and having heard from our friends there that we
had been daily looking for him, he had come to us
in London.   He and Mr. Gardiner were the two
surgeons, as mentioned in the former volume,
who had promised me, when I was in Bristol, in
the year 1787, that they would keep a journal
of facts for me during the voyages they were then
going to perform.   They had both of them kept
this promise.   Gardiner, I found, had died upon
the coast, and his journal, having been discovered
at his death, had been buried with him in great
triumph.   But Arnold had survived, and he came
now to offer us his services in the cause.

As it was a pity that such correct information as
that taken down in writing upon the spot should
be lost (for all the other evidences, except Dr.
Spaarman and Mr. Wadstrom, had spoken from
their memory only), I made all the interest I could
to procure a hearing for Mr. Arnold.   Pleading
now for the examination of him only, and under
these particular circumstances, I was attended to.
It was consented, in consequence of the little time
which was now left for preparing and printing the
Report, that I should make out his evidence from
his journal under certain heads.   This I did.   Mr.
Arnold swore to the truth of it, when so drawn
up, before Edward Montague, esquire, a master in
chancery.   He then delivered the paper in which
it was contained to the lords of the council, who,

on receiving it, read it throughout, and then questioned him upon it.

At this time, also, my brother returned with accounts and papers relative to the Slave-trade, from Havre de Grace ; but as I had pledged myself to offer no other person to be examined, his evidence was lost.   Thus, after all the pains we had taken, and in a contest, too, on the success of which our own reputation and the fate of Africa depended, we were obliged to fight the battle with sixteen less than we could have brought into the field ; while our opponents, on the other hand, on account of their superior advantages, had mustered all their forces, not having omitted a single man.

I do not know of any period of my life in which I suffered so much both in body and mind, as from the time of resuming these public inquiries by the privy council, to the time when they were closed. For I had my weekly duty to attend at the committee for the abolition during this interval.   I had to take down the examinations of all the evidences who came to London, and to make certain copies of these.   I had to summon these to town, and to make provision against all accidents ; and here I was often troubled by means of circumstances, which unexpectedly occurred, lest, when committees of the council had been purposely appointed to hear them, they should not be forthcoming at the time.   I had also a new and extensive correspondence to keep up ; for the tables of questions which had been sent down to our cor-

respondents, brought letters almost innumerable
on this subject, and they were always addressed
to me. These not only required answers of themselves, but as they usually related to persons capable of giving their testimony, and contained
the particulars of what they could state, they
occasioned fresh letters to be written to others.
Hence the writing of ten or twelve daily became
necessary.

But the contents of these letters afforded the
circumstances, which gave birth to so much suffering. They contained usually some affecting tale
of wo. At Bristol my feelings had been harassed
by the cruel treatment of the seamen, which had
come to my knowledge there : but now I was
doomed to see this treatment over again in many
other melancholy instances ; and additionally to
take in the various sufferings of the unhappy
slaves. These accounts I could seldom get time
to read till late in the evening, and sometimes not
till midnight, when the letters containing them
were to be answered. The effect of these accounts
was in some instances to overwhelm me for a time
in tears, and in others to produce a vivid indignation, which affected my whole frame. Recovering
from these, I walked up and down the room. I
felt fresh vigor, and made new determinations
of perpetual warfare against this impious trade.
I implored strength that I might proceed. I then
sat down, and continued my work as long as my
wearied eyes would permit me to see. Having
been agitated in this manner, I went to bed : but

my rest was frequently broken by the visions which floated before me. When I awoke, these renewed themselves to me, and they flitted about with me for the remainder of the day. Thus I was kept continually harassed : my mind was confined to one gloomy and heart-breaking subject for months. It had no respite, and my health began now materially to suffer.

But the contents of these letters were particularly grievous, on account of the severe labors, which they necessarily entailed upon me in other ways than those which have been mentioned. It was my duty, while the privy council examinations went on, not only to attend to all the evidence which was presented to us by our correspondents, but to find out and select the best. The happiness of millions depended upon it. Hence I was often obliged to travel during these examinations, in order to converse with those who had been pointed out to us as capable of giving their testimony ; and, that no time might be lost, to do this in the night. More than two hundred miles in a week were sometimes passed over on these occasions.

The disappointments, too, which I frequently experienced in these journeys, increased the poignancy of the suffering, which arose from a contemplation of the melancholy cases which I had thus travelled to bring forward to the public view. The reader at present can have no idea of these. I have been sixty miles to visit a person of whom I had heard, not only as possessing important knowledge, but as espousing our opinions on this subject. I have at length seen him. He has applauded my pursuit at our first interview. He has told me, in the course of our conversation, that neither my own pen, nor that of any other man, could describe adequately the horrors of the Slave-trade, horrors which he himself had witnessed. He has exhorted me to perseverance in this noble cause. Could I have wished for a more favorable reception? But mark the issue. He was the nearest relation of a rich person concerned in the traffic; and if he were to come forward with his evidence publicly, he should ruin all his expectations from that quarter. In the same week I have visited another at a still greater distance. I have met with similar applause. I have heard him describe scenes of misery which he had witnessed, and on the relation of which he himself almost wept. But mark the issue again. "I am a surgeon," says he; "through that window you see a spacious house. It is occupied by a West Indian. The medical attendance upon his family is of considerable importance to the temporal interests of mine. If I give you my evidence I lose his patronage. At the house above him lives an East Indian. The two families are connected: I fear, if I lose the support of one, I shall lose that of the other also: but I will give you privately all the intelligence in my power."

The reader may now conceive the many miserable hours I must have spent, after such visits, in returning home; and how grievously my heart

must have been afflicted by these cruel disappointments, but more · particularly where they arose
from causes inferior to those which have been
now mentioned, or from little frivolous excuses,
or idle and unfounded conjectures, unworthy of
beings expected to fill a moral station in life. Yes,
O man! often in these solitary journeyings have
I exclaimed against the baseness of thy nature, ·
when reflecting on the little paltry considerations
which have smothered thy benevolence, and hindered thee from succoring an oppressed brother.
And yet, on a further view of things, I have
reasoned myself into a kinder feeling, towards
thee. For I have been obliged to consider ultimately, that there were both lights and shades
in the human character; and that, if the bad
part of our nature was visible on these occasions,
the nobler part of it ought not to be forgotten.
While I passed a censure upon those, who were
backward in serving this great cause of humanity
and justice, how many did I know, who were
toiling in the support of it! I drew also this consolation from my reflections, that I had done my
duty; that I had left nothing untried or undone;
that amidst all these disappointments I had collected information, which might be useful at a
future time; and that such disappointments were
almost inseparable from the prosecution of a cause
of such magnitude, and where the interests of so
many were concerned.

Having now given a general account of my own
proceedings, I shall state those of the committee;

or show how they contributed, by fulfilling the
duties of their several departments, to promote
the cause in the interim.

In the first place they completed the rules, or
code of laws, for their own government.

They continued to adopt and circulate books,
that they might still enlighten the public mind
on the subject, and preserve it interested in favor
of their institution. They kept the press indeed
almost constantly going for this purpose. They
printed, within the period mentioned, Ramsay's
Address on the proposed Bill for the Abolition;
the Speech of Henry Beaufoy, esquire, on Sir
William Dolben's Bill, of which an extract was
given in the first volume; Notes by a Planter on
the two Reports from the Committee of the honorable House of Assembly of Jamaica; Observations on the Slave-trade by Mr. Wadstrom; and
Dickson's Letters on Slavery. These were all new
publications. To those they added others of less
note, with new editions of the old.

They voted their thanks to the reverend Mr.
Gifford, for his excellent sermon on the Slave-
trade; to the pastor and congregation of the Baptist church at Maze Pond, Southwark, for their
liberal subscription; and to John Barton, one of
their own members, for the services he had rendered them. The latter, having left his residence
in town for one in the country, solicited permission to resign, and hence this mark of approbation
was given to him. He was continued also as an
honorary and corresponding member.

They elected David Hartley and Richard Sharpe, esquires, into their own body, and Alexander Jaffray, esquire, the reverend Charles Symmons of Haverfordwest, and the reverend T. Burgess, (now bishop of St. David's) as honorary and corresponding members. The latter had written Considerations on the Abolition of Slavery and the Slave-trade upon grounds of natural, religious, and political duty, which had been of great service to the cause.

Of the new correspondents of the committee within this period I may first mention Henry Taylor, of North Shields; William Proud, of Hull; the reverend T. Gisborne, of Yoxall Lodge; and William Ellford, esquire, of Plymouth. The latter as chairman of the Plymouth committee, sent up for inspection an engraving of a plan and section of a slave-ship, in which the bodies of the slaves were seen stowed in the proportion of rather less than one to a ton. This happy invention gave all those, who saw it, a much better idea than they could otherwise have had of the horrors of their transportation, and contributed greatly as will appear afterwards, to impress the public in favor of our cause.

The next whom I shall mention, was C. L. Evans, esquire, of West Bromwich; the reverend T. Clarke, of Hull; S. P. Wolferstan, esquire, of Statford near Tamworth; Edmund Lodge, esquire, of Halifax; the reverend Caleb Rotheram, of Kendal; and Mr. Campbell Haliburton, of Edinburgh. The news which Mr. Haliburton sent was very

agreeable.   He informed us that, in consequence
of the great exertions of Mr. Alison, an institution had been formed in Edinburgh, similar to
that in London, which would take all Scotland
under its care and management, as far as related
to this great subject.   He mentioned lord Gar-
denston as the chairman; Sir William Forbes as
the deputy chairman; himself as the secretary;
and lord Napier, professor Andrew Hunter, professor Greenfield, and William Creech, Adam
Rolland, Alexander Ferguson, John Dickson,
John Erskine, John Campbell, Archibald Gib-
son, Archibald Fletcher, and Horatius Canning,
esquires, as the committee.

The others were the reverend J. Bidlake, of
Plymouth; Joseph Storrs, of Chesterfield; William Fothergill, of Carr End, Yorkshire; J. Sey-
mour, of Coventry; Moses Neave, of Poole; Joseph Taylor, of Scarborough; Timothy Clark, of
Doncaster; Thomas Davis, of Milverton; George
Croker Fox, of Falmouth; Benjamin Grubb, of
Clommell in Ireland; Sir William Forbes, of Edinburgh; the reverend J. Jamieson, of Forfar; and
Joseph Gurney, of Norwich; the latter of whom
sent up a remittance, and intelligence at the same
time, that a committee, under Mr. Leigh, so often
before mentioned, had been formed in that city.*

But the committee in London, while they were
endeavoring to promote the object of their insti-

---

* On the removal of Mr. Leigh from Norwich, Dr. Pretyman,
precentor of Lincoln, and a prebend of Norwich, succeeded him.

tution at home, continued their exertions for the same purpose abroad within this period.

They kept up a communication with the different societies established in America.

They directed their attention also to the continent of Europe. They had already applied, as I mentioned before, to the king of Sweden in favor of their cause, and had received a gracious answer. They now attempted to interest other potentates in it. For this purpose they bound up in an elegant manner two sets of the Essays on the Slavery and Commerce of the Human Species and on the Impolicy of the Slave-trade, and sent them to the Chevalier de Pinto, in Portugal. They bound up in a similar manner three sets of the same, and sent them to Mr. Eden, (now lord Auckland,) at Madrid, to be given to the king of Spain, the Count d'Aranda, and the Marquis del Campomanes.

They kept up their correspondence with the committee at Paris, which had greatly advanced itself in the eyes of the French nation; so that, when the different bailliages sent deputies to the States-General, they instructed them to take the Slave-trade into their consideration as a national object, and with a view to its abolition.

They kept up their correspondence with Dr. Frossard of Lyons. He had already published in France on the subject of the Slave-trade; and now he offered the committee to undertake the task, so long projected by them, of collecting such arguments and facts concerning it, and translating them into different languages, as might be useful in forwarding their views in foreign parts.

They addressed letters also to various individuals, to Monsieur Snetlage, doctor of laws at Halle in Saxony; to Monsieur Ladebat, of Bordeaux; to the Marquis de Feuillade d'Aubusson, at Paris; and to Monsieur Necker. The latter in his answer replied in part as follows: "As this great question," says he, "is not in my department, but in that of the minister for the colonies, I cannot interfere in it directly, but I will give indirectly all the assistance in my power. I have for a long time taken an interest in the general alarm on this occasion, and in the noble alliance of the friends of humanity in favor of the injured Africans. Such an attempt throws a new lustre over your nation. It is not yet, however, a national object in France. But the moment may perhaps come; and I shall think myself happy in preparing the way for it. You must be aware, however, of the difficulties which we shall have to encounter on our side of the water; for our colonies are much more considerable than yours; so that in the view of political interest we are not on an equal footing. It will therefore be necessary to find some middle line at first, as it cannot be expected that humanity alone will be the governing principle of mankind."

But the day was now drawing near, when it was expected that this great contest would be decided. Mr. Wilberforce on the nineteenth of March rose up in the House of Commons, and desired the

resolution to be read, by which the house stood
pledged to take the Slave-trade into their consideration in the then session.   He then moved that
the house should resolve itself into a committee of
the whole house on Thursday, the twenty-third of
April, for this purpose.   This motion was agreed
to ; after which he moved for certain official documents, necessary to throw light upon the subject
in the course of its discussion.

This motion, by means of which the great day
of trial was now fixed, seemed to be the signal for
the planters, merchants, and other interested persons to begin a furious opposition.   Meetings were
accordingly called by advertisement.   At these
meetings much warmth and virulence were manifested in debate, and propositions breathing a spirit
of anger were adopted.   It was suggested there, in
the vehemence of passion, that the islands could
exist independently of the mother country ; nor
were even threats withheld to intimidate government from effecting the abolition.

From this time, also, the public papers began
to be filled with such statements as were thought
most likely to influence the members of the House
of Commons, previously to the discussion of the
question.

The first impression attempted to be made upon
them was with respect to the slaves themselves.
It was contended, and attempted to be shown by
the revival of the old argument of human sacrifices
in Africa, that these were better off in the islands
than in their own country.   It was contended also,

that they were people of very inferior capacities, and but little removed from the brute creation; whence an inference was drawn, that their treatment, against which so much clamor had arisen, was adapted to their intellect and feelings.

The next attempt was to degrade the abolitionists in the opinion of the house, by showing the wildness and absurdity of their schemes. It was again insisted upon that emancipation was the real object of the former; so that thousands of slaves would be let loose in the islands to rob or perish, and who could never be brought back again into habits of useful industry.

An attempt was then made to excite their pity in behalf of the planters. The abolition, it was said, would produce insurrections among the slaves. But insurrections would produce the massacre of their masters;-and, if any of these should happily escape from butchery, they would be reserved only for ruin.

An appeal was then made to them on the ground of their own interest and of that of the people, whom they represented. It was stated that the ruin of the islands would be the ruin of themselves and of the country. Its revenue would be half annihilated. Its naval strength would decay. Merchants, manufacturers and others, would come to beggary. But in this deplorable situation they would expect to be indemnified for their losses. Compensation indeed must follow. It could not be withheld. But what would be the amount of it? The country would have no less than from eighty to a hundred millions to pay the sufferers; and it would be driven to such distress in paying this sum as it had never before experienced.

The last attempt was to show them that a regulation of the trade was all that was now wanted. While this would remedy the evils complained of, it would prevent the mischief which would assuredly follow the abolition. The planters had already done their part. The assemblies of the different islands had most of them made wholesome laws upon the subject. The very bills passed for this purpose in Jamaica and Grenada had arrived in England, and might be seen by the public: the great grievances had been redressed: no slave could now be mutilated or wantonly killed by his owner; one man could not now maltreat, or bruise, or wound the slave of another; the aged could not now be turned off to perish by hunger. There were laws also relative to the better feeding and clothing of the slaves. It remained only that the trade to Africa should be put under as wise and humane regulations as the slavery in the islands had undergone.

These different statements, appearing now in the public papers from day to day, began, in this early stage of the question, when the subject in all its bearings was known but to few, to make a considerable impression upon those, who were soon to be called to the decision of it. But that, which had the greatest effect upon them, was the enormous amount of the compensation, which, it was

said, must be made. This statement against the
abolition was making its way so powerfully, that
archdeacon Paley thought it his duty to write,
and to send to the committee, a little treatise
called Arguments against the Unjust Pretensions
of Slave Dealers and Holders, to be Indemnified
by Pecuniary Allowances at the Public Expense
in case the Slave-trade should be Abolished. This
treatise, when the substance of it was detailed in
the public papers, had its influence upon several
members of the House of Commons. But there
were others, who had been as it were panic-struck
by the statement. These in their fright seemed
to have lost the right use of their eyes, or to have
looked through a magnifying glass. With these
the argument of emancipation, which they would
have rejected at another time as ridiculous, obtained now easy credit. The massacres too and
the ruin, though only conjectural, they admitted
also. Hence some of them deserted our cause
wholly, while others, wishing to do justice as far
as they could to the slaves on the one hand, and
to their own countrymen on the other, adopted a
middle line of conduct, and would go no further
than the regulation of the trade.

While these preparations were making by our
opponents to prejudice the minds of those, who
were to be the judges in this contest, Mr. Pitt presented the privy council report at the bar of the
House of Commons; and as it was a large folio
volume, and contained the evidence upon which
the question was to be decided, it was necessary

that time should be given to the members to peruse it. Accordingly the twelfth of May was appointed, instead of the twenty-third of April, for the discussion of the question.

This postponement of the discussion of the question gave time to all parties to prepare themselves further.   The merchants and planters availed themselves of it to collect petitions to Parliament from interested persons against the abolition of the trade, to wait upon members of Parliament by deputation, in order to solicit their attendance in their favor, and to renew their injurious paragraphs in the public papers.   The committee for the abolition availed themselves of it to reply to these; and here Dr. Dickson, who had been secretary to governor Hey, in Barbadoes, and who had offered the committee his Letters on Slavery before mentioned, and his services also, was of singular use.   Many members of Parliament availed themselves of it to retire into the country to read the report.   Among the latter were Mr. Wilberforce and Mr. Pitt.   In this retirement they discovered, notwithstanding the great disadvantages under which we had labored with respect to evidence, that our cause was safe, and that as far as it was to be decided by reason and sound policy, it would triumph.   It was in this retirement that Mr. Pitt made those able calculations, which satisfied him for ever after, as the minister of the country, as to the safety of the great measure of the abolition of the Slave-trade; for he had clearly proved, that not only the islands could

go on in a flourishing state without supplies from·
the coast of Africa, but that they were then in a
condition to do it.

At length, the twelfth of May arrived. Mr.
Wilberforce rose up in the commons, and moved
the order of the day for the house to resolve itself
into a committee of the whole house, to take into
consideration the petitions, which had been presented against the Slave-trade.

This order having been read, he moved that
the report of the committee of privy council; that
the acts passed in the islands relative to slaves;
that the evidence adduced last year on the Slave-
trade; that the petitions offered in the last session
against the Slave-trade; and that the accounts
presented to the house, in the last and present
session, relative to the exports and imports to
Africa, be referred to the same committee.

These motions having been severally agreed
to, the house immediately resolved itself into a
committee of the whole house, and Sir William
Dolben was put into the chair.

Mr. Wilberforce began by declaring, that, when
he considered how much discussion the subject,
which he was about to explain to the committee,
had occasioned not only in that house but throughout the kingdom, and throughout Europe; and
when he considered the extent and importance of
it, the variety of interests involved in it, and the
consequences which might arise, he owned he
had been filled with apprehensions, lest a subject
of such magnitude, and a cause of such weight

should suffer from the weakness of its advocate;
but when he recollected that in the progress of his
inquiries he had everywhere been received with
candor, that most people gave him credit for the
purity of his motives, and that, however many of
these might then differ from him, they were all
likely to agree in the end, he had dismissed his
fears and marched forward with a firmer step in
this cause of humanity, justice and religion. He
could not, however, but lament that the subject
had excited so much warmth. He feared that
too many on this account were but ill prepared to
consider it with impartiality. He entreated all
such to endeavor to be calm and composed. A
fair and cool discussion was essentially necessary.
The motion he meant to offer was as reconcileable
to political expediency as to national humanity.
It belonged to no party question. It would in
the end be found serviceable to all parties; and
to the best interests of the country. He did not
come forward to accuse the West India planter,
or the Liverpool merchant, or indeed any one concerned in this traffic; but, if blame attached any
where, to take shame to himself, in common indeed with the whole Parliament of Great Britain,
who, having suffered it to be carried on under
their own authority, were all of them participators
in the guilt.

In endeavoring to explain the great business of
the day, he said he should call the attention of the
house only to the leading features of the Slave-
trade. Nor should he dwell long upon these.

Every one might imagine for himself, what must be the natural consequence of such a commerce with Africa. Was it not plain that she must suffer from it? that her savage manners must be rendered still more ferocious? and that a trade of this nature, carried on round her coasts, must extend violence and desolation to her very centre? It was well known that the natives of Africa were sold as goods, and that numbers of them were continually conveyed away from their country by the owners of British vessels. The question then was, which way the latter came by them. In answer to this question the privy council report, which was then on the table, afforded evidence the most satisfactory and conclusive. He had found things in it, which had confirmed every proposition he had maintained before, whether this proposition had been gathered from living information of the best authority, or from the histories he had read. But it was unnecessary either to quote the report, or to appeal to history on this occasion. Plain reason and common sense would point out how the poor Africans were obtained. Africa was a country divided into many kingdoms, which had different governments and laws. In many parts the princes were despotic. In others they had a limited rule. But in all of them, whatever the nature of the government was, men were considered as goods and property, and, as such, subject to plunder in the same manner as property in other countries. The persons in power there were naturally fond of our commodities; and to

obtain them (which could only be done by the
sale of their countrymen), they waged war on one
another, or even ravaged their own country, when
they could find no pretence for quarrelling with
their neighbors : in their courts of law many poor
wretches, who were innocent, were condemned;
and, to obtain these commodities in greater abun-
dance, thousands were kidnapped, and torn from
their families, and sent into slavery. Such transactions, he said, were recorded in every history
of Africa, and the report on the table confirmed
them. With respect, however, to these, he should
make but one or two observations. If we looked
into the reign of Henry the Eighth, we should
find a parallel for one of them. We should
find that similar convictions took place ; and that
penalties followed conviction. With respect to
wars, the kings of Africa were never induced to
engage in them by public principles, by national
glory, and least of all by the love of their people.
This had been stated by those most conversant in
the subject, by Dr. Spaarman and Mr. Wadstrom.
They had conversed with these princes, and had
learned from their own mouths, that to procure
slaves was the object of their hostilities. Indeed,
there was scarcely a single person examined before the privy council, who did not prove that the
Slave-trade was the source of the tragedies acted
upon that extensive continent. Some had endeavored to palliate this circumstance ; but there
was not one who did not more or less admit it to
be true. By one the Slave-trade was called the

concurrent cause, by the majority it was acknowledged to be the principal motive of the African
wars.   The same might be said with respect to
those instances of treachery and injustice, in which
individuals were concerned.   And here he was
sorry to observe that our own countrymen were
often guilty.   He would only at present advert to
the tragedy at Calabar, where two large African
villages, having been for some time at war, made
peace.   This peace was to have been ratified by
intermarriages ; but some of our captains, who
were there, seeing their trade would be stopped
for a while, sowed dissension again between them.
They actually set one village against the other,
took a share in the contest, massacred many of
the inhabitants, and carried others of them away
as slaves.   But shocking as this transaction might
appear, there was not a single history of Africa to
be read, in which scenes of as atrocious a nature
were not related.   They, he said, who defended
this trade, were warped and blinded by their own
interests, and would not be convinced of the miseries they were daily heaping on their fellow
creatures.   By the countenance they gave it, they
had reduced the inhabitants of Africa to a worse
state than that of the most barbarous nation.
They had destroyed what ought to have been the
bond of union and safety among them : they had
introduced discord and anarchy among them :
they had set kings against their subjects, and
subjects against each other : they had rendered
every private family wretched ; they had, in

short, given birth to scenes of injustice and misery
not to be found in any other quarter of the globe.

Having said thus much on the subject of procuring slaves in Africa, he would now go to that
of the transportation of them. And here he had
fondly hoped, that when men with affections and
feelings like our own had been torn from their
country, and every thing dear to them, he should
have found some mitigation of their sufferings:
but the sad reverse was the case. This was the
most wretched part of the whole subject. He was
incapable of impressing the house with what he
felt upon it. A description of their conveyance
was impossible. So much misery condensed in so
little room was more than the human imagination
had ever before conceived. Think only of six
hundred persons linked together, trying to get rid
of each other, crammed in a close vessel with
every object that was nauseous and disgusting,
diseased, and struggling with all the varieties of
wretchedness. It seemed impossible to add any
thing more to human misery. Yet shocking as
this description must be felt to be by every man,
the transportation had been described by several
witnesses from Liverpool to be a comfortable conveyance. Mr. Norris had painted the accommoda-
tions on board a slave-ship in the most glowing
colors. He had represented them in a manner
which would have exceeded his attempts at praise
of the most luxurious scenes. Their apartments,
he said, were fitted up as advantageously for them
as circumstances could possibly admit: they had

several meals a day; some, of their own country provisions, with the best sauces of African cookery; and, by way of variety, another meal of pulse, according to the European taste. After breakfast they had water to wash themselves, while their apartments were perfumed with frankincense and lime juice. Before dinner they were amused after the manner of their country: instruments of music were introduced: the song and the dance were promoted: games of chance were furnished them: the men played and sang, while the women and girls made fanciful ornaments from beads, with which they were plentifully supplied. They were indulged in all their little fancies, and kept in sprightly humor. Another of them had said, when the sailors were flogged, it was out of the hearing of the Africans, lest it should depress their spirits. He by no means wished to say that such descriptions were wilful misrepresentations. If they were not, it proved that interest or prejudice was capable of spreading a film over the eyes thick enough to occasion total blindness.

Others, however, and these men of the greatest veracity, had given a different account. What would the house think, when by the concurring testimony of these the true history was laid open? The slaves who had been described as rejoicing in their captivity, were so wrung with misery at leaving their country, that it was the constant practice to set sail in the night, lest they should know the moment of their departure. With respect to their accommodation, the right ankle of

one was fastened to the left ankle of another by
an iron fetter; and if they were turbulent, by
another on the wrists. Instead of the apartments
described, they were placed in niches, and along
the decks, in such a manner that it was impossible for any one to pass among them, however
careful he might be, without treading upon them.
Sir George Young had testified, that in a slave-
ship, on board of which he went, and which had
not completed her cargo by two hundred and fifty,
instead of the scent of frankincense being percep-
tible to the nostrils, the stench was intolerable.
The allowance of water was so deficient, that the
slaves were frequently found gasping for life, and
almost suffocated. The pulse with which they
had been said to be favored, were absolutely
English horsebeans. The legislature of Jamaica
had stated the scantiness both of water and provisions, as a subject which called for the interference of Parliament. As Mr. Norris had said,
the song and the dance were promoted, he could
not pass over these expressions without telling the
house what they meant. It would have been
much more fair if he himself had explained the
word *promoted*. The truth was, that, for the sake
of exercise, these miserable wretches, loaded with
chains and oppressed with disease, were forced to
dance by the terror of the lash, and sometimes
by the actual use of it. "I," said one of the evidences, "was employed to dance the men, while
another person danced the women." Such then
was the meaning of the word *promoted*; and it

might also be observed with respect to food, that
instruments were sometimes carried out, in order
to force them to eat; which was the same sort
of proof, how much they enjoyed themselves in
this instance also. With respect to their singing,
it consisted of songs of lamentation for the loss
of their country. While they sung they were in
tears: so that one of the captains, more humane
probably than the rest, threatened a woman with
a flogging because the mournfulness of her song
was too painful to his feelings. Perhaps he could
not give a better proof of the sufferings of these
injured people during their passage, than by stating the mortality which accompanied it. This was
a species of evidence which was infallible on this
occasion. Death was a witness which could not
deceive them; and the proportion of deaths would
not only confirm, but, if possible, even aggravate
our suspicion of the misery of the transit. It
would be found, upon an average of all the ships,
upon which evidence had been given, that, exclu-
sively of such as perished before they sailed from
Africa, not less than twelve and a half per cent.
died on their passage: besides these, the Jamaica
report stated that four and a half per cent. died
while in the harbors, or on shore before the day
of sale, which was only about the space of twelve
or fourteen days after their arrival there; and one
third more died in the seasoning; and this in a
climate exactly similar to their own, and where,
as some of the witnesses pretended, they were
healthy and happy. Thus, out of every lot of one

hundred, shipped from Africa, seventeen died in about nine weeks, and not more than fifty lived to become effective laborers in our islands.

Having advanced thus far in his investigation, he felt, he said, the wickedness of the Slave-trade to be so enormous, so dreadful, and irremediable, that he could stop at no alternative short of its abolition. A trade founded on iniquity, and carried on with such circumstances of horror, must be abolished, let the policy of it be what it might; and he had from this time determined, whatever were the consequences, that he would never rest till he had effected that abolition. His mind had indeed been harassed by the objections of the West India planters, who had asserted, that the ruin of their property must be the consequence of such a measure. He could not help, however, distrusting their arguments. He could not believe that the Almighty Being, who had forbidden the practice of rapine and bloodshed, had made rapine and bloodshed necessary to any part of his universe. He felt a confidence in this persuasion, and took the resolution to act upon it. Light indeed soon broke in upon him. The suspicion of his mind was every day confirmed by increasing information, and the evidence he had now to offer upon this point was decisive and complete. The principle upon which he founded the necessity of the abolition was not policy, but justice: but, though justice were the principle of the measure, yet he trusted he should distinctly prove it to be reconcileable with our truest political interest.

In the first place, he asserted that the number
of the slaves in our West India Islands might be
kept up without the introduction of recruits from
Africa; and to prove this, he would enumerate
the different sources of their mortality.   The first
was the disproportion of the sexes, there being,
upon an average, about five males imported to
three females: but this evil, when the Slave-trade
was abolished, would cure itself.   The second consisted in the bad condition in which they were
brought to the islands, and the methods of preparing them for sale.   They arrived frequently in
a sickly and disordered state, and then they were
made up for the market by the application of
astringents, washes, mercurial ointments, and re-
pelling drugs, so that their wounds and diseases
might be hid.   These artifices were not only fraud-
ulent but fatal: but these, it was obvious, would
of themselves fall with the trade.   A third was,
excessive labor joined with improper food; and a
fourth was, the extreme dissoluteness of their
manners.   These also would both of them be
counteracted by the impossibility of getting further
supplies: for owners, now unable to replace those
slaves whom they might lose, by speedy purchases
in the markets, would be more careful how they
treated them in future, and a better treatment
would be productive of better morals.   And here
he would just advert to an argument used against
those who complained of cruelty in our islands,
which was, that it was the interest of masters to
treat their slaves with humanity: but surely it

was immediate and present, not future and distant, interest, which was the great spring of action in the affairs of mankind.   Why did we make laws to punish men'?   It was their interest to be upright and virtuous : but there was a present impulse continually breaking in upon their better judgment, and an impulse, which was known to be contrary to their permanent advantage.   It was ridiculous to say that men would be bound by their interest, when gain or ardent passion urged them.   It might as well be asserted that a stone could not be thrown into the air, or a body move from place to place, because the principle of gravitation bound them to the surface of the earth. If a planter in the West Indies found himself reduced in his profits, he did not usually dispose of any part of his slaves ; and his own gratifications were never given up, so long as there was a possibility of making any retrenchment in the allowance of his slaves.   But to return to the subject which he had left : He was happy to state, that as all the causes of the decrease which he had stated might be remedied, so, by the progress of light and reformation, these remedies had been gradually coming into practice ; and that, as these had increased, the decrease of slaves had in an equal proportion been lessened.   By the gradual adoption of these remedies, he could prove from the report on the table, that the decrease of slaves in Jamaica had lessened to such a degree, that from the year 1774 to the present, it was not quite one in a hundred, and that in fact they were at

present in a state of increase ; for that the births
in that island, at this moment, exceeded the deaths
by one thousand or eleven hundred per annum.
Barbadoes, Nevis, Antigua, and the Bermudas,
were, like Jamaica, lessening their decrease, and
holding forth an evident and reasonable expectation of a speedy state of increase by natural population. But allowing the number of negroes even
to decrease for a time, there were methods which
would ensure the welfare of the West India islands.
The lands there might be cultivated by fewer
hands, and this to greater advantage to the proprietors and to this country, by the produce of cinnamon, coffee, and cotton, than by that of sugar.
The produce of the plantations, might also be
considerably increased, even in the case of sugar,
with less hands than were at present employed, if
the owners of them would but introduce machines
of husbandry. Mr. Long himself, long resident
as a planter, had proved, upon his own estate,
that the plough, though so little used in the West
Indies, did the service of a hundred slaves, and
caused the same ground to produce three hogs-
heads of sugar, which, when cultivated by slaves,
would only produce two. The divisions of work,
which, in free and civilized countries, was the
grand source of wealth, and the reduction of the
number of domestic servants, of whom not less
than from twenty to forty were kept in ordinary
families, afforded other resources for this purpose.
But, granting that all these suppositions should be
unfounded, and that every one of these substitutes

should fail for a time, the planters would be indemnified, as is the case in all transactions of commerce, by the increased price of their produce in the British market. Thus, by contending against the abolition, they were defeated in every part of the argument. But he would never give up the point, that the number of the slaves could be kept up by natural population, and without any dependance whatever on the Slave-trade. He therefore called upon the house again to abolish it as a criminal waste of life; it was utterly unnecessary; he had proved it so by documents contained in the report. The merchants of Liverpool, indeed, had thought otherwise, but he should be cautious how he assented to their opinions. They declared last year that it was a losing trade at two slaves to a ton, and yet they pursued it when restricted to five slaves to three tons. He believed, however, that it was upon the whole a losing concern; in the same manner as the lottery would be a losing adventure to any company who should buy all the tickets. Here and there an individual gained a large prize, but the majority of adventurers gained nothing. The same merchants, too, had asserted that the town of Liverpool would be ruined by the abolition. But Liverpool did not depend for its consequence upon the Slave-trade. The whole export tonnage from that place amounted to no less than 170,000 tons; whereas the export part of it to Africa amounted only to 13,000. Liverpool, he was sure, owed its greatness to other and

very different causes; the Slave-trade bearing but
a small proportion to its other trades.

Having gone through that part of the subject
which related to the slaves, he would now answer
two objections which he had frequently heard
started. The first of these was, that the abolition
of the Slave-trade would operate to the total ruin
of our navy, and to the increase of that of our
rivals. For an answer to these assertions, he
referred to what he considered to be the most valuable part of the report, and for which the house
and the country were indebted to the indefatigable
exertions of Mr. Clarkson. By the report it appeared that, instead of the Slave-trade being a
nursery for British seamen, it was their grave. It
appeared that more seamen died in that trade in
one·year than in the whole remaining trade of the
country in two. Out of nine hundred and ten
sailors in it, two hundred and sixteen died in the
year, while upon a fair average of the same number of men employed in the trades to the East
and West Indies, Petersburgh, Newfoundland, and
Greenland, no more than eighty-seven died. It
appeared, also, that out of three thousand one
hundred and seventy, who had left Liverpool in
the slave-ships in the year 1787, only one thousand
four hundred and twenty-eight had returned.
And here, while he lamented the loss which the
country thus annually sustained in her seamen,
he had additionally to lament the barbarous usage
which they experienced, and which this trade,
by its natural tendency to harden the heart, ex-

clusively produced. He would just read an extract of a letter from governor Parrey of Barbadoes, to lord Sydney, one of the secretaries of state. The governor declared he could no longer contain himself on account of the ill treatment, which the British sailors endured at the hands of their savage captains. These were obliged to have their vessels strongly manned, not only on account of the unhealthiness of the climate of Africa, but of the necessity of guarding the slaves, and preventing and suppressing insurrections; and when they arrived in the West Indies, and were out of all danger from the latter, they quarrelled with their men on the most frivolous pretences, on purpose to discharge them, and thus save the payment of supernumerary wages home. Thus many were left in a deceased and deplorable state; either to perish by sickness, or to enter into foreign service; great numbers of whom were for ever lost to their country. The governor concluded by declaring, that the enormities attendant on this trade were so great, as to demand the immediate interference of the legislature.

The next objection to the abolition was, that if we were to relinquish the Slave-trade, our rivals, the French, would take it up; so that, while we should suffer by the measure, the evil would still go on, and this even to its former extent. This was, indeed, a very weak argument; and, if it would defend the continuance of the Slave-trade, might equally be urged in favor of robbery, murder, and every species of wickedness, which, if

we did not practise, others would commit. But
suppose, for the sake of argument, that they were
to take it up, what good would it do them? What
advantages, for instance, would they derive from
this pestilential commerce to their marine? Should
not we, on the other hand, be benefited by this
change? Would they not be obliged to come to us,
in consequence of the cheapness of our manufactures, for what they wanted for the African market? But he would not calumniate the French
nation so much as to suppose that they would carry
on the trade if we were to relinquish it. He believed, on the other hand, that they would abolish
it also. Mr. Necker the present minister of France,
was a man of religious principle; and, in his
work upon the administration of the finances, had
recorded his abhorrence of this trade. He was
happy also to relate an anecdote of the present
king of France, which proved that he was a friend
to the abolition; for, being petitioned to dissolve
a society, formed at Paris, for the annihilation
of the slave-trade, his majesty answered, that he
would not, and was happy to hear that so humane
an association was formed in his dominions. And
here, having mentioned the society in Paris, he
could not help paying a due compliment to that
established in London for the same purpose, which
had labored with the greatest assiduity to make
this important subject understood, and which had
conducted itself with so much judgment and moderation as to have interested men of all religions,
and to have united them in their cause.

There was another topic which he would submit to the notice of the house before he concluded. They were perhaps not aware, that a fair and honorable trade might be substituted in the natural productions of Africa, so that our connexion with that continent in the way of commercial advantage need not be lost. The natives had already made some advances in it; and if they had not appeared so forward in raising and collecting their own produce for sale as in some other countries it was to be imputed to the Slave-trade; but remove the cause, and Africa would soon emerge from her present ignorant and indolent state. Civilization would go on with her as well as with other nations. Europe three or four centuries ago was in many parts as barbarous as Africa at present, and chargeable with as bad practices. For, what would be said, if, so late as the middle of the thirteenth century, he could find a parallel there for the Slave-trade? Yes. This parallel was to be found even in England. The people of Bristol, in the reign of Henry the Seventh, had a regular market for children, which were bought by the Irish: but the latter having experienced a general calamity, which they imputed as a judgment from heaven on account of this wicked traffic, abolished it. The only thing, therefore, which he had to solicit of the house, was to show that they were now as enlightened as the Irish were four centuries back, by refusing to buy the children of other nations. He hoped they would do it. He hoped, too, they would do it in an

unqualified manner. Nothing less than a total
abolition of the trade would do away the evils complained of. The legislature of Jamaica, indeed,
had thought that regulations might answer the
purpose. Their report had recommended, that no
person should be kidnapped, or permitted to be
made a slave, contrary to the customs of Africa.
But might he not be reduced to this state very
unjustly, and yet by no means contrary to the
African laws? Besides, how could we distinguish
between those who were justly or unjustly reduced to it? Could we discover them by their
physiognomy?—But if we could, who would believe that the British captains would be influenced
by any regulations made in this country, to refuse
to purchase those who had not been fairly, honestly, and uprightly enslaved? They who were
offered to us for sale were brought, some of them,
three or four thousand miles, and exchanged like
cattle from one hand to another, till they reached
the coast. But who could return these to their
homes, or make them compensation for their sufferings during their long journeyings? He would
now conclude by begging pardon of the house for
having detained them so long. He could indeed
have expressed his own conviction in fewer words.
He needed only to have made one or two short
statements, and to have quoted the command-
ment, "Thou shalt do no murder." But he
thought it his duty to lay the whole of the case,
and the whole of its guilt, before them. They
would see now that no mitigations, no palliatives,

would either be efficient or admissible. Nothing
short of an absolute abolition could be adopted.
This they owed to Africa: they owed it, too, to
their own moral characters. And he hoped they
would follow up the principle of one of the repent-
ant African captains, who had gone before the
committee of privy council as a voluntary witness
and that they would make Africa all the atone-
ment in their power for the multifarious injuries
she had received at the hands of British subjects.
With respect to these injuries, their enormity and
extent, it might be alleged in their excuse, that
they were not fully acquainted with them till that
moment, and therefore not answerable for their
former existence: but now they could no longer
plead ignorance concerning them. They had seen
them brought directly before their eyes, and they
must decide for themselves, and must justify to
the world and their own consciences the facts and
principles upon which their decision was formed.

Mr. Wilberforce having concluded his speech,
which lasted three hours and a half, read, and laid
on the table of the house, as subjects for their future discussion, twelve propositions, which he had
deduced from the evidence contained in the privy
council report, and of which the following is the
abridged substance:

1. That the number of slaves annually carried
from the coast of Africa, in British vessels, was
about 38,000, of which, on an average, 22,500
were carried to the British islands, and that of the
latter only 17,500 were retained there.

2. That these slaves, according to the evidence on the table, consisted, first, of prisoners of war; secondly, of free persons sold for debt, or on account of real or imputed crimes, particularly adultery and witchcraft; in which cases they were frequently sold with their whole families, and sometimes for the profit of those by whom they were condemned; thirdly, of domestic slaves sold for the profit of their masters, in some places at the will of the masters, and in others, on being condemned by them for real or imputed crimes; fourthly, of persons made slaves by various acts of oppression, violence, or fraud, committed either by the princes and chiefs of those countries on their subjects, or by private individuals on each other; or, lastly, by Europeans engaged in this traffic.

3. That the trade so carried on had necessarily a tendency to occasion frequent and cruel wars among the natives; to produce unjust convictions and punishments for pretended or aggravated crimes; to encourage acts of oppression, violence, and fraud, and to obstruct the natural course of civilization and improvement in those countries.

4. That Africa in its present state furnished several valuable articles of commerce which were partly peculiar to itself, but that it was adapted to the production of others, with which we were now either wholly or in great part supplied by foreign nations. That an extensive commerce with Africa might be substituted in these commodities, so as to afford a return for as many articles

as had annually been carried thither in British vessels : and, lastly, that such a commerce might reasonably be expected to increase by the progress of civilization there.

5. That the Slave-trade was peculiarly destructive to the seamen employed in it ; and that the mortality there had been much greater than in any British vessels employed upon the same coast in any other service or trade.

6. That the mode of transporting the slaves from Africa to the West Indies necessarily exposed them to many and grievous sufferings, for which no regulations could provide an adequate remedy ; and that in consequence thereof a large proportion had annually perished during the voyage.

7. That a large proportion had also perished in the harbors in the West Indies, from the diseases contracted in the voyage and the treatment of the same, previously to their being sold, and that this loss amounted to four and a half per cent. of the imported slaves.

8. That the loss of the newly imported slaves, within the three first years after their importation, bore a large proportion to the whole number imported.

9. That the natural increase of population among the slaves in the islands, appeared to have been impeded principally by the following causes: First, by the inequality of the sexes in the importations from Africa. Secondly, by the general dissoluteness of manners among the slaves, and the want of proper regulations for the encourage-

ment of marriages and of rearing children among
them. Thirdly, by the particular diseases which
were prevalent among them, and which were in
some instances to be attributed to too severe labor, or rigorous treatment, and in others to insufficient or improper food. Fourthly, by those diseases, which affected a large proportion of negro
children in their infancy, and by those, to which
the negroes newly imported from Africa had been
found to be particularly liable.

10. That the whole number of the slaves in the
island of Jamaica in 1768, was about 167,000, in
1774, about 193,000, and in 1787, about 256,000 :
that by comparing these numbers with the numbers imported and retained in the said island during all these years, and making proper allowances
the annual excess of deaths above births was in
the proportion of about seven-eighths per cent. ;
that in the first six years of this period it was in
the proportion of rather more than one on every
hundred ; that in the last thirteen years of the
same it was in the proportion of about three-
fifths on every hundred ; and that a number of
slaves, amounting to fifteen thousand, perished
during the latter period in consequence of repeated
hurricanes, and of the want of foreign supplies of
provisions.

11. That the whole number of slaves in the
island of Barbadoes was in the year 1764, about
70,706 ; in 1774, about 74,874 ; in 1780, about
68,270 ; in 1781, after the hurricane, about
63,248, and in 1786, about 62,115 : that by com-

paring these numbers with the number imported
into this island, (not allowing for any re-exporta-
tion,) the annual excess of deaths above births in
the ten years from 1764 to 1774, was in the proportion of about five on every hundred ; that in the
seven years from 1774 to 1780, it was in the proportion of about one and one-third on every hundred ; that between the year 1780 and 1781, there
had been a decrease in the number of slaves of
about five thousand ; that in the six years from
1781 to 1786, the excess of deaths was in the proportion of rather less than seven-eighths on every
hundred ; that in the four years from 1783 to
1786, it was in the proportion of rather less than
one-third on every hundred ; and that, during the
whole period, there was no doubt that some had
been exported from the island, but considerably
more in the first part of this period than in the
last.

12. That the accounts from the Leeward islands,
and from Dominica, Grenada, and St. Vincent's,
did not furnish sufficient grounds for comparing
the state of population in the said islands at different periods with the number of slaves, which
had been from time to time imported there and
exported therefrom ; but that from the evidence
which had been received respecting the present
state of these islands, as well as that of Jamaica
and Barbadoes, and from a consideration of the
means of obviating the causes, which had hitherto
operated to impede the natural increase of the
slaves, and of lessening the demand for manual

labor, without diminishing the profit of the planters, no considerable or permanent inconvenience would result from discontinuing the further importation of African slaves.

These propositions having been laid upon the table of the house, lord Penrhyn rose in behalf of the planters, and next after him, Mr. Gascoyne (both members for Liverpool), in behalf of the merchants concerned in the latter place. They both predicted the ruin and misery, which would inevitably follow the abolition of the trade. The former said, that no less than seventy millions were mortgaged upon lands in the West Indies, all of which would be lost. Mr. Wilberforce therefore should have made a motion to pledge the house to the repayment of this sum, before he had brought forward his propositions. Compensation ought to have been agreed upon as a previously necessary measure. The latter said, that in consequence of the bill of last year many ships were laid up and many seamen out of employ. His constituents had large capitals engaged in the trade, and if it were to be wholly done away, they would suffer from not knowing where to employ them. They both joined in asserting, that Mr. Wilberforce had made so many misrepresentations in all the branches of this subject, that no reliance whatever was to be placed on the picture which he had chosen to exhibit. They should speak, however, more fully to this point, when the propositions were discussed.

The latter declaration called up Mr. Wilber-

force again, who observed, that he had no intention of misrepresenting any fact. He did not
know that he had done it in any one instance;
but, if he had, it would be easy to convict him
out of the report upon the table.

Mr. Burke then rose. He would not, he said,
detain the committee long. Indeed he was not
able, weary and indisposed as he then felt himself,
even if he had an inclination to do it; but as, on
account of his other parliamentary duty, he might
not have it in his power to attend the business
now before them in its course, he would take that
opportunity of stating his opinion upon it.

And, first, the house, the nation, and all Europe
were under great obligations to Mr. Wilberforce
for having brought this important subject forward.
He had done it in a manner the most masterly,
impressive, and eloquent. He had laid down his
principles so admirably, and with so much order
and force, that his speech had equalled any thing
he had ever heard in modern oratory, and perhaps
it had not been excelled by any thing to be found
in ancient times. As to the Slave-trade itself,
there could not be two opinions about it where
men were not interested. A trade, begun in
savage war, prosecuted with unheard-of barbarity,
continued during the transportation with the most
loathsome imprisonment, and ending in perpetual
exile and slavery, was a trade so horrid in all its
circumstances, that it was impossible to produce
a single argument in its favor. On the ground
of prudence, nothing could be said in defence of

18*

it ; nor could it be justified by necessity. It was
necessity alone, that could be brought to justify
inhumanity ; but no case of necessity could be
made out strong enough to justify this monstrous
traffic. It was therefore the duty of the house to
put an end to it, and this without further delay.
This conviction, that it became them to do it immediately, made him regret (and it was the only
thing he regretted in the admirable speech he had
heard,) that his honorable friend should have introduced propositions on this subject. He could
have wished that the business had been brought
to a conclusion at once, without voting the propositions which had been read to them. He was
not over fond of abstract propositions. They were
seldom necessary ; and often occasioned great difficulty, embarrassment, and delay. There was
besides no occasion whatever to assign detailed
reasons for a vote, which nature herself dictated,
and which religion enforced. If it should happen,
that the propositions were not carried in that
house or the other, such a complication of mischiefs might follow, as might occasion them
heartily to lament that they were ever introduced.
If the ultimate resolution should happen to be
lost, he was afraid the propositions would pass as
waste paper, if not be injurious to the cause at a
future time.

And now, as the house must bring this matter
to an issue, he would beg their attention to a particular point. He entreated them to look further
than the present moment, and to ask themselves,

if they had fortified their minds sufficiently to bear the consequences, which might arise from the abolition of the Slave-trade, supposing they should decide upon it. When they abandoned it, other foreign powers might take it up, and clandestinely supply our islands with slaves. Had they virtue enough to see another country reaping profits, which they themselves had given up; and to abstain from that envy natural to rivals, and firmly to adhere to their determination; if so, let them thankfully proceed to vote the immediate abolition of the Slave-trade. But if they should repent of their virtue (and he had known miserable instances of such repentance), all hopes of future reformation of this enormous evil would be lost. They would go back to a trade they had abandoned with redoubled attachment, and would adhere to it with a degree of avidity and shameless ardor, to their own humiliation, and to the degradation and disgrace of the nation in the eyes of all Europe. These were considerations worth regarding, before they took a decisive step in a business, in which they ought not to move with any other determination than to abide by the consequences at all hazards. The honorable gentleman (who to his eternal honor had introduced this great subject to their notice) had in his eloquent oration knocked at every door, and appealed to every passion, well knowing that mankind were governed by their sympathies. But there were other passions to be regarded. Men were always ready to obey their sympathies, when it cost them nothing. But were they prepared to pay the price of their virtue on this great occasion? This was the question. If they were, they would do themselves immortal honor, and would have the satisfaction of having done away a commerce, which, while it was productive of misery not to be described, most of all hardened the heart, and vitiated the human character.

With respect to the consequences mentioned by the two members for Liverpool, he had a word or two to offer upon them. Lord Penrhyn had talked of millions to be lost and paid for. But seeing no probability of any loss ultimately, he could see no necessity for compensation. He believed, on the other hand, that the planters would be great gainers by those wholesome regulations, which they would be obliged to make, if the Slave-trade were abolished. He did not, however, flatter them with the idea that this gain would be immediate. Perhaps they might experience inconveniences at first, and even some loss. But what then? With their loss, their virtue would be the greater. And in this light he hoped the house would consider the matter; for, if they were called upon to do an act of virtuous energy and heroism, they ought to think it right to submit to temporary disadvantages for the sake of truth, justice, humanity, and the prospect of greater happiness.

The other member, Mr. Gascoyne, had said, that his constituents, if the trade were abolished, could not employ their capitals elsewhere. But

whether they could or not, it was the duty of
that house, if they put them into a traffic, which
was shocking to humanity and disgraceful to the
nation, to change their application, and not to
allow them to be used to a barbarous purpose.
He believed, however, that the merchants of Liverpool would find no difficulty on this head. All
capitals required active motion. It was in their
nature not to remain passive and unemployed.
They would soon turn them into other channels.
This they had done themselves during the American war; for the Slave-trade was then almost
wholly lost, and yet they had their ships employed,
either as transports in the service of government,
or in other ways.

And as he now called upon the house not to
allow any conjectural losses to become impedi-
ments in the way of the abolition of the Slave-
trade, so he called upon them to beware how they
suffered any representations of the happiness of
the state of slavery in our islands to influence
them against so glorious a measure. Admiral
Barrington had said in his testimony, that he had
often envied the condition of the slaves there.
But surely, the honorable admiral must have
meant, that, as he had often toiled like a slave in
the defence of his country, (as his many gallant
actions had proved,) so he envied the day, when
he was to toil in a similar manner in the same
cause. If, however, his words were to be taken
literally, his sensations could only be accounted
for by his having seen the negroes in the hour of

their sports, when a sense of the misery of their condition was neither felt by themselves nor visible to others.   But their appearance on such occasions did by no means disprove their low and abject state.   Nothing made a happy slave but a degraded man.   In proportion as the mind grows callous to its degradation, and all sense of manly pride is lost, the slave feels comfort.   In fact, he is no longer a man.   If he were to define a man, he would say with Shakspeare,

> "Man is a being holding large discourse,
> Looking before and after."

But a slave was incapable of looking before and after.   He had no motive to do it.   He was a mere passive instrument in the hands of others, to be used at their discretion.   Though living, he was dead as to all voluntary agency.   Though moving amidst the creation with an erect form, and with the shape and semblance of a human being, he was a nullity as a man.

Mr. Pitt thanked his honorable friend Mr. Wilberforce for having at length introduced this great and important subject to the consideration of the house.   He thanked him also for the perspicuous, forcible, and masterly manner, in which he had treated it.   He was sure that no argument, compatible with any idea of justice, could be assigned for the continuation of the Slave-trade.   And, at the same time that he was willing to listen with candor and attention to every thing that could be urged on the other side of the question, he was sure that the principles from which his opinion was deduced were unalterable. He had examined the subject with the anxiety which became him, where the happiness and interests of so many thousands were concerned, and with the minuteness which would be expected of him, on account of the responsible situation which he held; and he averred, that it was sophistry, obscurity of ideas, and vagueness of reasoning, which alone could have hitherto prevented all mankind (those immediately interested in the question excepted,) from agreeing in one and the same opinion upon the subject. With respect to the propriety of introducing the individual propositions which had been offered, he differed with Mr. Burke, and he thanked his honorable friend Mr. Wilberforce for having chosen the only way in which it could be made obvious to the world, that they were warranted on every ground of reason and of fact in coming to that vote, which he trusted would be the end of their proceeding. The grounds for the attainment of this end were distinctly stated in the propositions. Let the propositions be brought before the house, one by one, and argued from the evidence; and it would then be seen, that they were such as no one, who was not deaf to the language of reason, could deny. Let them be once entered upon the journals of that house, and it was almost impossible they should fail. The abolition must be voted. As to the mode of it, or how it should be effected, they were not at present to discuss it; but he trusted it would be such as would not invite foreign powers to supply our islands with slaves by a clandestine trade.

After a debt, founded on the immutable principles of justice, was found to be due, it was impossible but the country had means to cause it to be paid. Should such an illicit proceeding be attempted, the only language which it became us to adopt was, that Great Britain had resources to enable her to protect her islands, and to prevent that traffic from being clandestinely carried on by them, which she had thought fit from a regard to her character to abandon. It was highly becoming Great Britain to take the lead of other nations in such a virtuous and magnificent measure, and he could not but have confidence, that they would be inclined to share the honor with us, or be pleased to follow us as their example. If we were disposed to set about this glorious work in earnest, they might be invited to concur with us by a negotiation to be immediately opened for that purpose. He would only now observe, before he sat down, in answer to certain ideas thrown out, that he could by no means acquiesce in any compensation for losses, which might be sustained by the people of Liverpool, or by others in any other part of the kingdom, in the execution of this just and necessary undertaking.

Sir William Yonge said, he wanted no inducement to concur with the honorable mover of the propositions, provided the latter could be fairly established, and no serious mischiefs were to arise from the abolition. But he was apprehensive that

ıy evils might follow, in the case of any sudl or unlooked-for decrease in the slaves. They
ıght be destroyed by hurricanes. They might
ıe swept off by many fatal disorders. In these
cases, the owners of them would not be able to
fill up their places, and they who had lent money
upon the lands, where the losses had happened,
would foreclose their mortgages. He was fearful,
also that a clandestine trade would be carried on,
and then the sufferings of the Africans, crammed
up in small vessels, which would be obliged to be
hovering about from day to day, to watch an opportunity of landing, would be ten times greater
than any which they now experienced in the legal
trade. He was glad, however, as the matter was
to be discussed, that it had been brought forward in the shape of distinct propositions, to be
grounded upon the evidence in the privy council
report.

Mr. Fox observed, that he did not like, where
he agreed as to the substance of a measure, to
differ with respect to the form of it. If, however,
he differed in any thing in the present case, it was
with a view rather to forward the business than
to injure it, or to throw any thing like an obstacle
in its way. Nothing like either should come from
him. What he thought was, that all the propositions were not necessary to be voted previously to
the ultimate decision, though some of them undoubtedly were. He considered them as of two
classes: the one, alleging the grounds upon which
it was proper to proceed to the abolition ; such as

that the trade was productive of inexpressible misery, in various ways, to the innocent natives of Africa; that it was the grave of our seamen; and so on: the other, merely answering objections which might be started, and where there might be a difference of opinion. He was however glad that the propositions were likely to be entered upon the journals; since, if from any misfortune, the business should be deferred, it might succeed another year. Sure he was that it could not fail to succeed sooner or later. He highly approved of what Mr. Pitt had said, relative to the language it became us to hold out to foreign powers in case of a clandestine trade. With respect, however, to the assertion of Sir William Yonge, that a clandestine trade in slaves would be worse than a legal one, he could not admit it. Such a trade, if it existed at all, ought only to be clandestine. A trade in human flesh and sinews was so scandalous, that it ought not openly to be carried on by any government whatever, and much less by that of a Christian country. With regard to the regulation of the Slave-trade, he knew of no such thing as a regulation of robbery and murder. There was no medium. The legislature must either abolish it, or plead guilty of all the wickedness which had been shown to attend it. He would now say a word or two with respect to the conduct of foreign nations on this subject. It was possible that these, when they heard that the matter had been discussed in that house, might follow the example, or they might go before us and set one themselves. If this were to happen, though we might be the losers, humanity would be the gainer. He himself had been thought sometimes to use expressions relative to France, which were too harsh, and as if he could only treat her as the enemy of this country. Politically speaking, France was our rival. But he well knew the distinction between political enmity and illiberal prejudice. If there was any great and enlightened nation in Europe, it was France, which was as likely as any country upon the face of the globe to catch a spark from the light of our fire, and to act upon the present subject with warmth and enthusiasm. France had often been improperly stimulated by her ambition; and he had no doubt but that, in the present instance, she would readily follow its honorable dictates.

Mr. (now lord) Grenville would not detain the house by going into a question, which had been so ably argued; but he should not do justice to his feelings, if he did not express publicly to his honorable friend, Mr. Wilberforce, the pleasure he had received from one of the most masterly and eloquent speeches he had ever heard; a speech, which, while it did honor to him, entitled him to the thanks of the house, of the people of England, of all Europe, and of the latest posterity. He approved of the proposition, as the best mode of bringing this great question to a happy issue. He was pleased also with the language which had been held out with respect to foreign nations, and with our determination to

assert our right of preventing our colonies from
carrying on any trade, which we had thought it
our duty to abandon.

Aldermen Newnham, Sawbridge, and Watson,
though they wished well to the cause of humanity, could not, as representatives of the city of
London, give their concurrence to a measure,
which would injure it so essentially as that of the
abolition of the Slave-trade. This trade might
undoubtedly be put under wholesome regulations,
and made productive of great commercial advantages. But, if it were abolished, it would render
the city of London one scene of bankruptcy and
ruin. It became the house to take care, while
they were giving way to the goodness of their
hearts, that they did not contribute to the ruin of
the mercantile interests of the country.

Mr. Martin stated, that he was so well satisfied
with the speech of the honorable gentlemen, who
had introduced the propositions, and with the language held out by other distinguished members
on this subject, that he felt himself more proud
than ever of being an Englishman. He hoped
and believed, that the melancholy predictions of
the worthy aldermen would not prove true, and
that the citizens of London would have too much
public spirit to wish that a great national object
(which comprehended the great duties of humanity and justice), should be set aside, merely
out of consideration to their own private interests.

Mr. Dempster expected, notwithstanding all he
had heard, that the first proposition submitted

to them, would have been to make good out of
the public purse all the losses individuals were
liable to sustain from an abolition of the Slave-
trade. This ought to have been, as lord Penrhyn
had observed, a preliminary measure. He did
not like to be generous out of the pockets of
others. They were to abolish the trade, it was
said, out of a principle of humanity. Undoubtedly they owed humanity to all mankind. But
they also owed justice to those who were interested
in the event of the question, and had embarked
their fortunes on the faith of Parliament. In fact,
he did not like to see men introducing even their
schemes of benevolence to the detriment of other
people; and much less did he like to see them
going to the colonies, as it were upon their estates,
and prescribing rules to them for their management. With respect to his own speculative opinion, as it regarded cultivation, he had no objection to give it. He was sure that sugar could be
raised cheaper by free men than by slaves. This
the practice in China abundantly proved. But
yet neither he nor any other person had a right
to force a system upon others. As to the trade
itself, by which the present laborers were supplied, it had been considered by that house as so
valuable, that they had preferred it to all others,
and had annually voted a considerable sum towards carrying it on. They had hitherto deemed
it an essential nursery for our seamen. Had it
really been such as had been represented, our
ancestors would scarcely have encouraged it; and
19 *

therefore, upon these and other considerations, he could not help thinking that they would be wanting in their duty, if they abolished it altogether.

Mr. William Smith would not detain the house long at that late hour upon this important subject; but he could not help testifying the great satisfaction he felt at the manner in which the honorable gentleman who opened the debate (if it could be so called,) had treated it. He approved of the propositions as the best mode of bringing the decision to a happy issue. He gave Mr. Fox great credit for the open and manly way, in which he had manifested his abhorrence of this trade, and for the support he meant to give to the total and unqualified abolition of it; for he was satisfied, that the more it was inquired into, the more it would be found that nothing short of abolition would cure the evil. With respect to certain assertions of the members for Liverpool, and certain melancholy predictions about the consequences of such an event, which others had held out, he desired to lay in his claim for observation upon them, when the great question should come before the house.

Soon after this the house broke up; and the discussion of the propositions, which was the next parliamentary measure intended, was postponed to a future day, which was sufficiently distant to give all the parties concerned time to make the necessary preparations for it.

Of this interval the committee for the abolition availed themselves to thank Mr. Wilberforce for

the very able and satisfactory manner in which
he had stated to the house his propositions for
the abolition of the Slave-trade, and for the unpar-
alleled assiduity and perseverance with which
he had all along endeavored to accomplish this
object, as well as to take measures themselves for
the further promotion of it. Their opponents
availed themselves of this interval also. But that
which now embarrassed them, was the evidence
contained in the privy council report. They had
no idea, considering the number of witnesses they
had sent to be examined, that this evidence,
when duly weighed, could by right reasoning
have given birth to the sentiments, which had
been displayed in the speeches of the most distinguished members of the House of Commons,
or to the contents of the propositions, which had
been laid upon their table. They were thunder-
struck as it were by their own weakness: and
from this time they were determined, if possible, to
get rid of it as a standard for decision, or to inter-
pose every parliamentary delay in their power.

On the twenty-first of May, the subject came
again before the attention of the house. It was
ushered in, as was expected, by petitions collected
in the interim, and which were expressive of the
frightful consequences which would attend the
abolition of the Slave-trade. Alderman Newnham
presented one from certain merchants in London;
alderman Watson another from certain merchants,
mortgagees, and creditors of the sugar islands; lord
Maitland another from the planters of Antigua;

Mr. Blackburne another from certain manufac‑
turers of Manchester; Mr. Gascoyne another from
the corporation of Liverpool; and lord Penrhyn
and others from different interested bodies in the
same town.

Mr. Wilberforce then moved the order of the
day, for the house to go into a committee of the
whole house on the report of the privy council,
and the several matters of evidence already upon
the table relative to the Slave-trade.

Mr. Alderman Sawbridge immediately arose,
and asked Mr. Wilberforce, if he meant to adduce
any other evidence, besides that in the privy
council report, in behalf of his propositions, or to
admit other witnesses, if such could be found, to
invalidate them. Mr. Wilberforce replied, that
he was quite satisfied with the report on the table.
It would establish all his propositions. He should
call no witnesses himself: as to permission to
others to call them, that must be determined by
the house.

This question and this answer gave birth imme‑
diately to great disputes upon the subject. Alder‑
men Sawbridge, Newnham, and Watson; lords
Penrhyn and Maitland; Mr. Gascoyne, Marsham,
and others spoke against the admission of the evi‑
dence, which had been laid upon the table. They
contended, that it was insufficient, defective, and
contradictory; that it was *ex parte* evidence; that
it had been manufactured by ministers; that it was
founded chiefly on hearsay, and that the greatest
part of it was false; that it had undergone no

cross-examination; that it was unconstitutional; and that, if they admitted it, they would establish a dangerous precedent, and abandon their rights. It was urged on the other hand by Mr. Courtenay, that it could not be *ex parte* evidence, because it contained testimony on both sides of the question. The circumstance also of its being contradictory, which had been alleged against it, proved that it was the result of an impartial examination. Mr. Fox observed, that it was perfectly admissible. He called upon those who took the other side of the question, to say why, if it was really inadmissible, they had not opposed it at first. It had now been a long time on the table, and no fault had been found with it. The truth was, it did not suit them, and they were determined by a side wind as it were, to put an end to the inquiry. Mr. Pitt observed that, if Parliament had previously resolved to receive no evidence on a given subject but from the privy council, such a resolution, indeed, would strike at the root of the privileges of the House of Commons; but it was absurd to suppose that the house could upon no occasion receive evidence, taken where it was most convenient to take it, and subject throughout to new investigation, if any one doubted its validity. The report of the privy council consisted, first, of calculations and accounts from the public offices, and next, of written documents on the subject; both of which were just as authentic, as if they had been laid upon the table of that house. The remaining part of it consisted of the testimony of living witnesses, all of whose names were published, so that if any one doubted their veracity, it was open to him to re-examine all or each of them. It had been said by adversaries that the report on the table was a weak and imperfect report, but would not these have the advantage of its weakness and imperfection? It was strange, when his honorable friend, Mr. Wilberforce, had said, "Weak and imperfect as the report may be thought to be, I think it strong enough to bear me out in all my propositions," that they, who objected to it, should have no better reason to give than this, "We object, because the ground of evidence on which you rest is too weak to support your cause." Unless it were meant to say, (and the meaning seemed to be but thinly disguised,) that the house ought to abandon the inquiry, he saw no reason whatever for not going immediately into a committee; and he wished gentlemen to consider whether it became the dignity, of their proceedings to obstruct the progress of an inquiry, which the house had pledged itself to undertake. Their conduct, indeed, seemed extraordinary on this occasion. It was certainly singular that, while the report had been five weeks upon the table, no argument had been brought against its sufficiency; but that on the moment when the house was expected to come to an ultimate vote upon the subject, it should be thought defective, contradictory, unconstitutional, and otherwise objectionable. These objections, he was satisfied, neither did nor could originate with the

country gentlemen; but they were brought forward, for purposes not now to be concealed, by the
avowed enemies of this noble cause.

In the course of the discussion, which arose
upon this subject, every opportunity was taken to
impress the house with the dreadful consequences
of the abolition. Mr. Henniker read a long letter
from the king of Dahomey to George the First,
which had been found among the papers of James
first duke of Chandos, and which had remained
in the family till that time. In this, the king of
Dahomey boasted of his victory over the king of
Ardrah, and how he had ornamented the pave-
ment and walls of his palace with the heads of
the vanquished. These cruelties, Mr. Henniker
said, were not imputable to the Slave-trade. They
showed the Africans to be naturally a savage
people, and that we did them a great kindness by
taking them from their country. Alderman Sawbridge maintained that, if the abolition passed, the
Africans, who could not be sold as slaves, would
be butchered at home; while those, who had been
carried to our islands, would be no longer under
control. Hence insurrections, and the manifold
evils which belonged to them. Alderman Newnham was certain that the abolition would be the
ruin of the trade of the country. It would affect
even the landed interest, and the funds. It would
be impossible to collect money to diminish the
national debt. Every man in the kingdom would
feel the abolition come home to him. Alderman
Watson maintained the same argument, and pro-

nounced the trade under discussion to be a merciful and humane trade.

Compensation was also insisted upon by Mr. Drake, Alderman Newnham, Mr. Henniker, Mr. Cruger, and others. This was resisted by Mr. Burke; who said that compensation in such a case would be contrary to every principle of legislation. Government gave encouragement to any branch of commerce, while it was regarded as conducive to the welfare of the community, or compatible with humanity and justice. But they were competent to withdraw their countenance from it, when it was found to be immoral, and injurious, and disgraceful to the state. They who engaged in it, knew the terms under which they were placed, and adopted it with all the risks with which it was accompanied; and of consequence it was but just, that they should be prepared to abide by the loss which might accrue, when the public should think it right no longer to support it. But such a trade as this it was impossible any longer to support. Indeed it was not a trade. It was a system of robbery. It was a system, too, injurious to the welfare of other nations. How could Africa ever be civilized under it? While we continued to purchase the natives, they must remain in a state of barbarism. It was impossible to civilize slaves. It was contrary to the system of human nature. There was no country placed under such disadvantageous circumstances, into which the shadow of improvement had ever been introduced.

Great pains were taken to impress the house with the propriety of regulation. Sir Grey Cooper; Aldermen Sawbridge, Watson and Newnham; Mr. Marsham, and Mr. Cruger, contended strenuously for it instead of abolition. It was also stated that the merchants would consent to any regulation of the trade, which might be offered them.

In the course of the debate much warmth of temper was manifested on both sides. The expression of Mr. Fox in a former debate, " that the Slave-trade could not be regulated, because there could be no regulation of robbery and murder," was brought up, and construed by planters in the house as a charge of these crimes upon themselves. Mr. Fox, however, would not retract the expression. He repeated it. He had no notion, however, that any individual would have taken it to himself. If it contained any reflection at all, it was on the whole Parliament, who had sanctioned such a trade. Mr. Molyneux rose up, and animadverted severely on the character of Mr. Ramsay, one of the evidences in the privy council report, during his residence in the West Indies. This called up Sir William Dolben and Sir Charles Middleton in his defence, the latter of whom bore honorable testimony to his virtues from an intimate acquaintance with him, and a residence in the same village with him, for twenty years. Mr. Molyneux spoke also in angry terms of the measure of abolition. To annihilate the trade, he said, and to make no compensation on account

of it, was an act of swindling.   Mr. Macnamara
called the measure hypocritical, fanatic, and meth-
odistical.   Mr. Pitt was so irritated at the insidious
attempt to set aside the privy council report, when
no complaint had been alleged against it before,
that he was quite off his guard, and he thought it
right afterwards to apologize for the warmth into
which he had been betrayed.   The speaker, too,
was obliged frequently to interfere.   On this occasion no less than thirty members spoke.   And
there had probably been few seasons, when so
much disorder had been discoverable in that house.

The result of the debate was, a permission to
those interested in the continuance of the Slave-
trade to bring counsel to the bar on the twenty-
sixth of May, and then to introduce such witnesses, as might throw further light on the propositions in the shortest time : for Mr. Pitt only
acquiesced in this new measure on a supposition,
"that there would be no unnecessary delay, as he
could by no means submit to the ultimate procrastination of so important a business."   He even
hoped (and in this hope he was joined by Mr. Fox),
that those concerned would endeavor to bring the
whole of the evidence they meant to offer at the
first examination.

On the day appointed, the house met for the
purposes now specified ; when alderman Newnham, thinking that such an important question
should not be decided but in a full assembly of
the representatives of the nation moved for a call
of the house on that day fortnight.   Mr. Wilber-

force stated that he had no objection to such a measure; believing the greater the number present the more favorable it would be to his cause. This motion, however, produced a debate and a division, in which it appeared that there were one hundred and fifty-eight in favor of it, and twenty-eight against it. The business of the day now commenced. The house went into a committee, and Sir William Dolben was put into the chair. Mr. Serjeant Le Blanc was then called in. He made an able speech in behalf of his clients, and introduced John Barnes, esquire, as his first witness, whose examination took up the remainder of the day. By this step they who were interested in the continuance of the trade, attained their wishes, for they had now got possession of the ground with their evidence; and they knew they could keep it, almost as long as they pleased, for the purposes of delay. Thus they, who boasted, when the privy council examinations began, that they would soon do-away all the idle tales which had been invented against them, and who desired the public only to suspend their judgment till the report should come out, when they would see the folly and wickedness of all our allegations, dared not abide by the evidence, which they themselves had taught others to look up to as the standard by which they were desirous of being judged: thus they, who had advantages beyond measure in forming a body of evidence in their own favor, abandoned that which they had collected. And here it is impossible for me not to make a short

comparative statement on this subject, if it were
only to show how little can be made out, with
the very best opportunities, against the cause of
humanity and religion. With respect to ourselves,
we had almost all our witnesses to seek. We had
to travel after them for weeks together. When
we found them, we had scarcely the power of
choice. We were obliged to take them as they
came. When we found them, too, we had generally to implore them to come forward in our
behalf. Of those so implored three out of four
refused, and the plea for this refusal was a fear
lest they should injure their own interest. The
merchants, on the other hand, had their witnesses
ready on the spot. They had always ships in
harbor containing persons, who had a knowledge
of the subject. They had several also from
whom to choose. If one man was favorable to
their cause in three of the points belonging to it,
but was unfavorable in the fourth, he could be
put aside and replaced. When they had thus
selected them, they had not to entreat, but to command, their attendance. They had no fear, again,
when they thus commanded, of a refusal on the
ground of interest; because these were promoting
their interest by obliging those who employed
them. Viewing these and other circumstances,
which might be thrown into this comparative
statement, it was some consolation to us to know,
amidst the disappointment which this new measure occasioned, and our apparent defeat in the
eyes of the public, that we had really beaten our

opponents at their own weapons, and that, as this
was a victory in our own private feelings, so it
was the presage to us of a future triumph.

On the twenty-ninth of May, Mr. Tierney made
a motion to divide the consideration of the Slave-
trade into two heads, by separating the African
from the West Indian part of the question. This
he did for the more clear discussion of the propositions, as well as to save time. This motion,
however, was overruled by Mr. Pitt.

At length, on the ninth of June, by which time
it was supposed that new light, and this in sufficient quantity, would have been thrown upon the
propositions, it appeared that only two witnesses
had been fully heard. The examinations, therefore, were continued, and they went on till the
twenty-third. On this day, the order for the call
of the house, which had been prolonged, standing
unrepealed, there was a large attendance of members. A motion was then made to get rid of the
business altogether, but it failed. It was now
seen, however, that it was impossible to bring the
question to a final decision in this session, for
they, who were interested in it, affirmed that they
had yet many important witnesses to introduce.
Alderman Newnham, therefore, by the consent of
Mr. Wilberforce, moved, that "the further consideration of the subject be deferred to the next
session." On this occasion, Mr. William Smith
remarked, that though the decision on the great
question was thus to be adjourned, he hoped the
examinations, at least, would be permitted to go

on. He had not heard any good reason why they might not be carried on for some weeks longer. It was known that the hearing of evidence was at all times thinly attended. If therefore the few members, who did attend, were willing to give up their time a little longer, why should other members complain of an inconvenience in the suffering of which they took no share ? He thought, that by this proceeding the examination of witnesses on the part of the merchants might be finished, and of consequence the business brought into a very desirable state of forwardness against the ensuing session. These observations had not the desired effect, and the motion of Mr. Alderman Newnham was carried without a division. Thus the great question, for the elucidation of which all the new evidences were to be heard at the very first examination, in order that it might be decided by the ninth of June, was, by the intrigue of our opponents deferred to another year.

The order of the day for going into the further consideration of the Slave-trade having been discharged, Sir William Dolben rose to state, that it was his intention to renew his bill of the former year, relative to the conveyance of the unhappy Africans from their own country to the West Indies, and to propose certain alterations in it. He made a motion accordingly, which was adopted ; and he and Mr. Wilberforce were desired to prepare the same.

This bill he introduced soon afterwards, and it passed ; but not without opposition. It was a

matter, however, of great pleasure to find that
the worthy baronet was enabled by the assistance
of captain (afterwards admiral) Macbride, and
other naval officers in the house, to carry such
clauses, as provided in some degree for the comfort of the poor seamen, who were seduced into
this wicked trade. They could not, indeed, provide against the barbarity of their captains; but
they secured them a space under the half deck in
which to sleep. They prescribed a form of muster-
rolls, which they were to see and sign in the
presence of the clearing officer. They regulated
their food both as to kind and quantity; and they
preserved them from many of the impositions to
which they had been before exposed.

From the time when Mr. Wilberforce gave his
first notice this session to the present, I had been
variously employed, but more particularly in the
composition of a new work. It was soon perceived to be the object of our opponents, to impress upon the public the preference of regulation
to abolition. I attempted therefore to show the
fallacy and wickedness of this notion. I divided
the evils belonging to the Slave-trade into two
kinds. These I enumerated in their order. With
respect to those of the first kind, I proved that
they were never to be remedied by any acts of
the British Parliament. Thus, for instance, what
bill could alter the nature of the human passions?
What bill could prevent fraud and violence in
Africa, while the Slave-trade existed there? What
bill could prevent the miserable victims of the

trade from rising, when on board the ships, if they saw an opportunity, and felt a keen sense of their oppression? Those of the second I stated to admit of a remedy, and, after making accurate calculations on the subject of each, I showed that those merchants, who were to do them away effectually, would be ruined by their voyages. The work was called An Essay on the Comparative Efficiency of Regulation or Abolition as applied to the Slave-trade.

The committee also, in this interval brought out their famous print of the plan and section of a slave-ship; which was designed to give the spectator an idea of the sufferings of the Africans in the middle passage, and this so familiarly, that he might instantly pronounce upon the miseries experienced there. The committee at Plymouth had been the first to suggest the idea; but that in London had now improved it. As this print seemed to make an instantaneous impression of horror upon all who saw it, and as it was therefore very instrumental, in consequence of the wide circulation given it, in serving the cause of the injured Africans, I have given the reader a copy of it in the annexed plate, and I will now state the ground or basis, upon which it was formed.

It must be obvious that it became the committee to select some one ship, which had been engaged in the Slave-trade, with her real dimensions, if they meant to make a fair representation of the manner of the transportation. When Captain Parry of the royal navy, returned from

Liverpool, to which place government had sent
him, he brought with him the admeasurement
of several vessels, which had been so employed,
and laid them on the table of the House of Commons. At the top of his list stood the ship Brookes.
The committee, therefore, in choosing a vessel on
this occasion made use of the ship Brookes; and
this they did, because they thought it less objectionable to take the first that came, than any
other. The vessel then in the plate is the vessel
now mentioned, and the following is her admeasurement as given in by Captain Parry.

	Ft.	In.
Length of the lower deck, gratings, and bulkheads in- cluded at A A, ...	100	0
Breadth of beam on the lower deck inside, B B, . .	25	4
Depth of hold O O O, from ceiling to ceiling, . .	10	0
Height between decks from deck to deck, . . .	5	8
Length of the men's room, C C, on the lower deck, .	46	0
Breadth of the men's room, C C, on the lower deck, .	25	4
Length of the platform, D D, in the men's room, . .	46	0
Breadth of the platform, in the men's room, on each side,	6	0
Length of the boys' room, E E, ...	13	9
Breadth of the boys' room, ...	25	0
Breadth of platform, F F, in boys' room, . . .	6	0
Length of women's room, G G, ...	28	6
Breadth of women's room, ...	23	6
Length of platform, H H, in women's room, . .	28	6
Breadth of platform in women's room, . . .	6	0
Length of the gun-room, I I, on the lower deck, . .	10	6
Breadth of the gun-room on the lower deck, . .	12	0
Length of the quarter deck, K K, ...	33	6
Breadth of the quarter deck, ...	19	6
Length of the cabin, L L, ...	14	0
Height of the cabin, ...	6	2
Length of the half deck, M M, ...	16	6
Height of the half deck, ...	6	2

Ft. In.

Length of the platform, N N, on the half deck, . . 16 6
Breadth of the platform on the half deck, . . . 6 0
Upper deck, P P. .

The committee having proceeded thus far,
thought that they should now allow certain
dimensions for every man, woman and child ; and
then see how many persons, upon such dimensions and upon the admeasurements just given,
could be stowed in this vessel. They allowed,
accordingly, to every man slave six feet by one
foot four inches for room, to every woman five
feet by one foot four, to every boy five feet by
one foot two, and to every girl four feet six by
one foot. They then stowed them, and found
them as in the annexed plate, that is, they found
(deducting the women stowed in Z of figures 6
and 7, which spaces, being half of the half deck,
were allowed by Sir William Dolben's last bill to
the seamen), that only four hundred and fifty
could be stowed in her, and the reader will find,
if he should think it worth while to count the
figures in the plate, that, on making the deduction mentioned, they will amount to this number.

The committee then thought it right to inquire
how many slaves the act of Sir William Dolben
allowed this vessel to carry, and they found the
number to be four hundred and fifty-four ; that is,
they found it allowed her to carry four more than
could be put in without trespassing upon the room
allotted to the rest ; for we see that the bodies of
the slaves, except just at the head of the vessel,

already touch each other, and that no deduction has been made for tubs or stanchions to support the platforms and decks.

Such was the picture which the committee were obliged to draw, if they regarded mathematical accuracy, of the room allotted to the slaves in this vessel. By this picture was exhibited the nature of the elysium, which Mr. Norris and others had invented for them during their transportation from their own country. By this picture were seen also the advantages of Sir William Dolben's bill; for many, on looking at the plate, considered the regulation itself as perfect barbarism. The advantages, however, obtained by it were considerable; for the Brookes was now restricted to four hundred and fifty slaves, whereas it was proved that she carried six hundred and nine in a former voyage.

The committee, at the conclusion of the session of Parliament, made a suitable report. It will be unnecessary to detail this for obvious reasons. There was, however, one thing contained in it, which ought not to be omitted. It stated, with appropriate concern, the death of the first controversial writer, and of one of the most able and indefatigable laborers in their cause. Mr. Ramsay had been for some time indisposed. The climate of the West Indies, during a residence of twenty years, and the agitation in which his mind had been kept for the last four years of his life, in consequence of the virulent attacks on his word and character by those interested in the continuance of the trade, had contibuted to undermine his constitution. During his whole illness he was cheerful and composed ; nor did he allow it to hinder him, severe as it was, from taking any opportunity which afforded of serving those unhappy persons, for whose injuries he had so deeply felt. A few days only before he died, I received from him probably the last letter he ever wrote, of which the following is an extract :—

"My health has certainly taken a most alarming turn ; and if some considerable alteration does not take place for the better in a very little time, it will be all over with me ; I mean as to the present life. I have lost all appetite ; and suffer grievously from an almost continual pain in my stomach, which leaves me no enjoyment of myself, but such as I can collect from my own reflections, and the comforts of religion. I am glad the bill for the abolition is in such forwardness. Whether it goes through the house or not, the discussion attending it will have a most beneficial effect. The whole of this business I think now to be in such a train, as to enable me to bid farewell to the present scene with the satisfaction of not having lived in vain, and of having done something towards the improvement of our common nature ; and this at no little expense of time and reputation. The little I have now written is my utmost effort ; yet yesterday I thought it necessary to write an answer to a scurrilous libel in The Diary by one Scipio. On my own account he should have remained unnoticed, but our great cause must be kept unsullied."

Mr. Ramsay was a man of active habit, of diligence and perseverance in his undertakings, and of extraordinary application. He was of mild and humble manners. He possessed a strong understanding, with great coolness and courage. Patriotism and public spirit were striking traits in his character. In domestic life he was amiable: in the ministry, exemplary and useful ; and he died to the great regret of his parishioners, but most of all to that of those who moved with him in his attempts to bring about the important event of the abolition of the Slave-trade.

CHAPTER IX.

CONTINUATION FROM JULY 1789 TO JULY 1790.—AUTHOR TRAVELS TO PARIS TO PROMOTE THE ABOLITION IN FRANCE—ATTENDS THE COMMITTEES OF THE FRIENDS OF THE NEGROES—COUNTER ATTEMPTS OF THE COMMITTEE OF WHITE COLONISTS—AN ACCOUNT OF THE DEPUTIES OF COLOR—MEETING AT THE DUKE DE LA ROCHEFOUCAULD'S—MIRABEAU ESPOUSES THE CAUSE—CANVASSES THE NATIONAL ASSEMBLY.—DISTRIBUTION OF THE SECTION OF THE SLAVE-SHIP THERE.—CHARACTER OF BRISSOT.—AUTHOR LEAVES PARIS AND RETURNS TO ENGLAND—EXAMINATION OF MERCHANTS' AND PLANTERS' EVIDENCE RESUMED IN THE HOUSE OF COMMONS.—AUTHOR TRAVELS IN SEARCH OF EVIDENCE IN FAVOR OF THE ABOLITION—OPPOSITION TO A HEARING OF IT—THIS EVIDENCE IS AT LENGTH INTRODUCED—RENEWAL OF SIR WILLIAM DOLBEN'S BILL—DISTRIBUTION OF THE SECTION OF THE SLAVE-SHIP IN ENGLAND—AND OF COWPER'S NEGRO'S COMPLAINT—AND OF WEDGWOOD'S CAMEOS.

WE usually find, as we give ourselves up to reflection, some little mitigation of the afflictions we experience ; and yet of the evils which come upon us, some are often so heavy as to overpower the sources of consolation for a time, and to leave us wretched. This was nearly our situation at the close of the last session of Parliament. It would be idle not to confess that circumstances had occurred, which wounded us deeply. Though we had foiled our opponents at their own weapons, and had experienced the uninterrupted good wishes and support of the public, we had the great mortification to see the enthusiasm of members of Parliament beginning to cool ; to see a question of humanity and justice (for such it was, when it was delivered into their hands), verging towards that of commercial calculation; and finally to see regulation, as it related to it, in the way of being substituted for abolition. But most of all were we affected knowing as we did the nature and the extent of the sufferings belonging to the Slave-trade, that these should be continued to another year. This last consideration almost overpowered me. It had fallen to my lot, more than to that of any other person, to know these evils, and I seemed almost inconsolable at the postponement of the question. I wondered how members of Parliament, and these Englishmen, could talk as they did on this subject; how they could bear for a moment to consider their fellow man as an article of trade; and how they should not count even the delay of an hour, which occasioned so much misery, to continue, as one of the most criminal actions of their lives.

It was in vain, however, to sink under our burthens. Grief could do no good; and if our affairs had taken an unfavorable turn, the question was, how to restore them. It was sufficiently obvious that, if our opponents were left to themselves, or, without any counteracting evidence, they would considerably soften down the propositions, if not invalidate them in the minds of many. They had such a power of selection of witnesses, that they could bring men forward, who might say with truth, that they had seen but very few of the evils complained of, and those in an inferior degree. We knew also from the example of the Liverpool delegates, how interest and prejudice could blind the eyes, and how others might be called upon to give their testimony, who would dwell upon the comforts of the Africans, when they came into our power; on the sprinkling of their apartments with frankincense; on the promotion of music and the dance among them; and on the health and festivity of their voyages. It seemed therefore necessary, that we should again be looking out for evidence on the part of the abolition. Nor did it seem to me to be unreasonable, if our opponents were allowed to come forward in a new way, because it was more constitutional, that we should be allowed the same privilege. By these means the evidence, of which we had now lost the use, might be restored; indifference might be fanned into warmth; commercial calculation might be overpowered by justice; and abolition, rising above the reach of the cry of regulation, might eventually triumph.

I communicated my ideas to the committee, and offered to go round the kingdom to accomplish this object. The committee had themselves been considering what measures to take, and as each in his own mind had come to conclusions similar with my own, my proposal was no sooner made, than adopted.

I had not been long upon this journey, when I was called back. Mr. Wilberforce, always solicitous for the good of this great cause, was of opinion, that, as commotions had taken place in France, which then aimed at political reforms, it was possible that the leading persons concerned in them might, if an application were made to them judiciously, be induced to take the Slave-trade into their consideration, and incorporate it among the abuses to be done away. Such a measure, if realized, would not only lessen the quantity of human suffering, but annihilate a powerful political argument against us. He had a conference therefore with the committee on this subject; and, as they accorded with his opinion, they united with him in writing a letter to me, to know if I would change my journey, and proceed to France.

As I had no object in view but the good of the cause, it was immaterial to me where I went, if I could but serve it; and therefore, without any further delay, I returned to London.

As accounts had arrived in England of the excesses which had taken place in the city of Paris, and of the agitated state of the provinces through which I was to pass, I was desired by several of my friends to change my name. To this I could not consent; and, on consulting the committee, they were decidedly against it.

I was introduced as quickly as possible, on my arrival at Paris, to the friends of the cause there, to the Duke de la Rochefoucauld, the Marquis de Condorcet, Messieurs Petion de Villeneuve, Claviere, and Brissot, and to the Marquis de la Fayette. The latter received me with peculiar marks of attention. He had long felt for the wrongs of Africa, and had done much to prevent them. He had a plantation in Cayenne, and had

21 *

devised a plan, by which the laborers upon it
should pass by degrees from slavery to freedom.
With this view he had there laid it down as a
principle, that all crimes were equal, whether they
were committed by blacks or whites, and ought
equally to be punished.   As the human mind is
of such a nature, as to be acted upon by rewards
as well as punishments, he thought it unreasonable, that the slaves should have no advantage
from a stimulus from the former.   He laid it
down therefore as another principle, that temporal
profits should follow virtuous actions.   To this he
subjoined a reasonable education to be gradually
given.   By introducing such principles, and by
making various regulations for the protection and
comforts of the slaves, he thought he could prove
to the planters, that there was no necessity for the
Slave-trade ; that the slaves upon all their estates
would increase sufficiently by population ; that
they might be introduced gradually, and without
detriment, to a state of freedom ; and that then
the real interests of all would be most promoted.
This system he had begun to act upon two years
before I saw him.   He had also, when the society
was established in Paris, which took the name
of The Friends of the Negroes, enrolled himself
a member of it.

The first public steps taken after my arrival in
Paris were at a committee of the Friends of the
Negroes, which was but thinly attended.   None
of those mentioned, except Brissot, were present.
It was resolved there, that the committee should

solicit an audience of M. Necker; and that I should wait upon him, accompanied by a deputation consisting of the Marquis de Condorcet, Monsieur de Bourge, and Brissot de Warwille: Secondly, that the committee should write to the president of the National Assembly, and request the favor of him to appoint a day for hearing the cause of the negroes; and, thirdly, that it should be recommended to the committee in London to draw up a petition to the National Assembly of France, praying for the abolition of the Slave-trade by that country. This petition, it was observed, was to be signed by as great a number of the friends to the cause in England, as could be procured. It was then to be sent to the committee at Paris, who would take it in a body to the place of its destination.

I found great delicacy as a stranger in making my observations upon these resolutions, and yet I thought I ought not to pass them over wholly in silence, but particularly the last. I therefore rose up, and stated that there was one resolution, of which I did not quite see the propriety. But this might arise from my ignorance of the customs, as well as of the genius and spirit of the French people. It struck me that an application from a little committee in England to the National Assembly of France was not a dignified measure, nor was it likely to have weight with such a body. It was, besides, contrary to all the habits of propriety, in which I had been educated. The British Parliament did not usually receive petitions from

the subjects of other nations.   It was this feeling,
which had induced me thus to speak.

To these observations it was replied, that the
National Assembly of France would glory in going
contrary to the example of other nations in a case
of generosity and justice, and that the petition in
question, if it could be obtained, would have an
influence there, which the people of England,
unacquainted with the sentiments of the French
nation, would hardly credit.

To this I had only to reply, that I would communicate the measure to the committee in London,
but that I could not be answerable for the part
they would take in it.

By an answer received from M. Necker, relative to the first of these resolutions, it appeared
that the desired interview had been obtained : but
he granted it only for a few minutes, and this
principally to show his good-will to the cause.
For he was then so oppressed with business in his
own department, that he had but little time for
any other.   He wrote to me, however, the next
day, and desired my company to dinner.   He
then expressed a wish to me, that any business
relative to the Slave-trade might be managed by
ourselves as individuals, and that I would take
the opportunity of dining with him occasionally
for this purpose.   By this plan, he said, both
of us would save time.   Madame Necker also
promised to represent her husband, if I should
call in his absence, and to receive me, and converse with me on all occasions, in which this

great cause of humanity and religion might be concerned.

With respect to the other resolutions nothing ever came of them ; for we waited daily for an answer from the president during the whole of his presidency, but we never received any ; and the committee in London, when they had read my letter, desired me unequivocally to say, that they did not see the propriety of the petition, which it had been recommended to them to obtain.

At the next meeting it was resolved, that a letter should be written to the new president for the same purpose as the former. This it was said, was now rendered essentially necessary. For the merchants, planters, and others interested in the continuance of the Slave-trade, were so alarmed at the enthusiasm of the French people, in favor of the new order of things, and of any change recommended to them, which had the appearance of promoting the cause of liberty, that they held daily committees to watch and to thwart the motions of the friends of the negroes. It was therefore thought proper, that the appeal to the Assembly should be immediate on this subject, before the feelings of the people should cool, or, before they, who were thus interested, should poison their minds by calculations of loss and gain. The silence of the former president was already attributed to the intrigues of the planters' committee. No time therefore was to be lost. The letter was accordingly written, but as no answer was ever returned to it, they attributed this second omission to the same cause.

I do not really know whether interested persons ever did, as was suspected, intercept the letters of the committee to the two presidents as now surmised; or whether they ever dissuaded them from introducing so important a question for discussion when the nation was in such a heated state; but certain it is that we had many, and I believe barbarous, enemies to encounter. At the very next meeting of the committee, Clavière produced anonymous letters, which he had received, and in which it was stated that, if the society of the Friends of the Negroes did not dissolve itself, he and the rest of them would be stabbed. It was said that no less than three hundred persons had associated themselves for this purpose. I had received similar letters myself; and on producing mine, and comparing the handwriting in both, it appeared that the same persons had written them.

In a few days after this the public prints were filled with the most malicious representations of the views of the committee. One of them was, that they were going to send twelve thousand muskets to the negroes in St. Domingo, in order to promote an insurrection there. This declaration was so industriously circulated, that a guard of soldiers was sent to search the committee room; but these were soon satisfied, when they found only two or three books and some waste paper. Reports equally unfounded and wicked were spread also in the same papers relative to myself. My

name was mentioned at full length, and the place.
of my abode hinted at.   It was stated at one
time, that I had proposed such wild and mischievous plans to the committee in London relative to
the abolition of the Slave-trade, that they had
cast me out of their own body, and that I had
taken refuge in Paris, where I now tried to impose.
equally on the French nation.   It was stated at
another, that I was employed by the British government as a spy, and that it was my object to
try to undermine the noble constitution, which
was then forming for France.   This latter report
at this particular time, when the passions of men.
were so inflamed, and when the stones of Paris
had not been long purified from the blood of Fou-
lon and Berthier, might have cost me my life;
and I mentioned it to General la Fayette, and
solicited his advice.   He desired me to make a.
public reply to it: which I did.   He desired me
also to change my lodging to the Hotel de York,
that I might be nearer to him; and to send to
him if there should be any appearance of a collection of people about the hotel, and I should
have aid from the military in his quarter.   He
said also, that he would immediately give in my.
name to the municipality; and that he would
pledge himself to them, that my views were
strictly honorable.

On dining one day at the house of the Marquis
de la Fayette, I met the deputies of color.   They
had arrived only the preceding day from St. Domingo.   I was desired to take my seat at dinner

in the midst of them. They were six in number;
of a sallow or swarthy complexion, but yet it was
not darker than that of some of the natives of the
south of France. They were already in the uni-
form of the Parisian National Guards; and one
of them wore the cross of St. Louis. They were
men of genteel appearance and modest behaviour.
They seemed to be well informed, and of a more
solid cast than those whom I was in the habit of
seeing daily in this city. The account which they
gave of themselves was this. The white people
of St. Domingo, consisting of less than ten thousand persons, had deputies then sitting in the
National Assembly. The people of color in the
same island greatly exceeded the white in number. They amounted to thirty thousand, and
were generally proprietors of lands. They were
equally free by law with the former, and paid their
taxes to the mother country in an equal proportion. But in consequence of having sprung from
slaves they had no legislative power, and moreover were treated with great contempt. Believing
that the mother country was going to make a
change in its political constitution, they had called
a meeting on the island, and this meeting had
deputed them to repair to France, and to desire
the full rights of citizens, or that the free people
of color might be put upon an equality with the
whites. They (the deputies) had come in consequence. They had brought with them a present
of six millions of livres to the National Assembly,
and an appointment to General la Fayette to be

commander in chief over their constituents, as a
distinct body. This command they said the general had accepted, though he had declined similar
honors from every town in France, except Paris,
in order to show that he patronised their cause.

I was now very anxious to know the sentiments
which these gentlemen entertained on the subject
of the Slave-trade. If they were with us, they
might be very useful to us; not only by their votes
in the Assembly, but by the knowledge of facts,
which they would be able to adduce there in our
favor. If they were against us, it became me
to be upon my guard against them, and to take
measures accordingly. I therefore stated to them
at once the nature of my errand to France, and
desired their opinion upon it. This they gave me
without reserve. They broke out into lavish com-
mendations of my conduct, and called me their
friend. The Slave-trade, they said, was the parent of all the miseries in St. Domingo, not only
on account of the cruel treatment it occasioned to
the slaves, but on account of the discord which it
constantly kept up between the whites and people
of color, in consequence of the hateful distinctions
it introduced. These distinctions could never be
obliterated while it lasted. Indeed both the trade
and the slavery must fall, before the infamy now
fixed upon a skin of color could be so done away,
that whites and blacks could meet cordially, and
look with respect upon one another. They had it
in their instructions, in case they should obtain a
seat in the Assembly, to propose an immediate

abolition of the Slave-trade, and an immediate
amelioration of the state of slavery also, with a
view to its final abolition in fifteen years.

But time was flying apace, I had now been
nearly seven weeks in Paris; and had done nothing. The thought of this made me uneasy, and
I saw no consoling prospect before me. I found it
even difficult to obtain a meeting of the Friends
of the Negroes. The Marquis de la Fayette had
no time to attend. Those of the committee, who
were members of the National Assembly, were
almost constantly engaged at Versailles. Such
of them as belonged to the municipality, had
enough to do at the Hotel de Ville. Others were
employed either in learning the use of arms, or in
keeping their daily and nightly guards. These
circumstances made me almost despair of doing
any thing for the cause at Paris, at least in any
reasonable time. But a new circumstance occurred, which distressed me greatly; for I discovered, in the most satisfactory manner, that two
out of the six at the last committee were spies.
They had come into the society for no other reason, than to watch and report its motions, and
they were in direct correspondence with the slave
merchants at Havre de Grace. This matter I
brought home to them afterwards, and I had the
pleasure of seeing them excluded from all our
future meetings.

From this time I thought it expedient to depend
less upon the committee and more upon my own
exertions, and I formed the resolution of going

among the members of the National Assembly
myself, and of learning from their own mouths
the hope I ought to entertain relative to the decision of our question. In the course of my endeavors I obtained a promise from the Duke de la
Rochefoucauld, the Comte de Mirabeau, the Abbé
Syeyes, Monsieur Bergasse, and Monsieur Petion
de Villeneuve, five of the most approved members
of the National Assembly, that they would meet
me, if I would fix a day. I obtained a similar
promise from the Marquis de Condorcet, and Claviere and Brissot, as members selected from the
committee of the Friends of the Negroes. And
Messieurs de Roveray and Du Monde, two Gene-
vese gentlemen at Versailles, men of considerable
knowledge and interest, and who had heard of
our intended meeting, were to join us at their
own request. The place chosen was the house
of the bishop of Chartres at Versailles.

I was now in hope that I should soon bring the
question to some issue ; and on the fourth of October I went to dine with the bishop of Chartres
to fix the day. We appointed the seventh. But
how soon, frequently, do our prospects fade ! From
the conversation which took place at dinner, I
began to fear that our meeting would not be realized. About three days before, the officers of
the Guard du Corps had given the memorable
banquet, recorded in the annals of the revolution,
to the officers of the regiment of Flanders which
then lay at Versailles. This was a topic, on which
the company present dwelt. They condemned it

as a most fatal measure in these heated times; and were apprehensive that something would grow immediately out of it, which might endanger the king's safety. In passing afterwards through the streets of Versailles my fears increased. I met several of that regiment in groups. Some were brandishing their swords. Others were walking arm in arm, and singing tumultuously. Others were standing and conversing earnestly together. Among the latter I heard one declare with great vehemence, "that it should not be; that the revolution must go on." On my arrival at Paris in the evening the Palais Royale was full of people, and there were movements and buzzings among them, as if something was expected to happen. The next day, when I went into the streets it was obvious what was going to take place. Suffice it to say, that the next evening the king and queen were brought prisoners into Paris. After this, things were in such an unsettled state for a few days, and the members of the National Assembly were so occupied in the consideration of the event itself, and of the consequences which might attend it, that my little meeting, of which it had cost me so much time and trouble to procure the appointment, was entirely prevented.

I had now to wait patiently till a new opportunity should occur. The Comte de Mirabeau, before the departure of the king, had moved and carried the resolution that "the assembly was inseparable from his majesty's person." It was expected, therefore, that the National Assembly would immediately transfer its sittings to Paris. This took place on the nineteenth. It was now more easy for me to bring persons together, than when I had to travel backward and forward to Versailles. Accordingly, by watching my opportunities, I obtained the promise of another meeting. This was held afterward at the Duke de la Rochefoucauld's. The persons before mentioned were present; except the Comte de Mirabeau, whose occupations at that moment made it utterly impossible for him to attend.

The duke opened the business in an appropriate manner; and concluded, by desiring each person to give his opinion frankly and unequivocally as to what might be expected of the National Assembly relative to the great measure of the abolition of the Slave-trade.

The Abbé Syeyes rose up, and said, it would probably bring the business within a shorter compass, if, instead of discussing this proposition at large, I were to put to the meeting my own questions. I accordingly accepted this offer; and began by asking those present "how long it was likely that the present National Assembly would sit?" After some conversation it was replied, that, "it would sit till it had completed the constitution, and interwoven such fixed principles into it, that the legislature, which should succeed it, might have nothing more to do, than to proceed on the ordinary business of the state. Its dissolution would probably not take place till the month of March."

22*

I then asked them, "whether it was their opinion, that the National Assembly would feel itself authorized to take up such a foreign question (if I might be allowed the expression), as that of the abolition of the Slave-trade?" The answer to this was, "that the object of the National Assembly was undoubtedly the formation of a constitution for the French people. With respect to foreign possessions, it was very doubtful, whether it were the real interest of France to have any colonies at all. But while it kept such colonies under its dominion, the assembly would feel, that it had the right to take up this question; and that the question itself would naturally spring out of the bill of rights, which had already been adopted as the basis of the constitution."

The next question I proposed was, "whether they were of opinion, that the National Assembly would do more wisely, in the present situation of things, to determine upon the abolition of the Slave-trade now, or to transfer it to the legislature, which was to succeed it in the month of March."

This question gave birth to a long discussion, during which much eloquence was displayed. But the unanimous answer, with the reason for it, may be conveyed in substance as follows. "It would be most wise, it was said, in the present assembly to introduce the question to the notice of the nation, and this as essentially connected with the bill of rights, but to transfer the determination of it, in a way the best calculated to ensure success, to the succeeding legislature. The revolution was of more importance to Frenchmen, than the abolition of the Slave-trade. To secure this was their first object, and more particularly, because the other would naturally flow from it. But the revolution might be injured by the immediate determination of the question. Many persons in the large towns of Bordeaux, Marseilles, Rouen, Nantes, and Havre, who were now friends to it, might be converted into enemies. It would also be held up by those, who wished to produce a counter revolution (and the ignorant and prejudiced might believe it), that the assembly had made a great sacrifice to England, by thus giving her an opportunity of enlarging her trade. The English House of Commons had taken up the subject, but had done nothing. And though they, who were then present, were convinced of the sincerity of the English minister, who had introduced it; and that the trade must ultimately fall in England, yet it would not be easy to persuade many bigoted persons in France of these truths. It would therefore be most wise in the assembly only to introduce the subject as mentioned; but if extraordinary circumstances should arise, such as a decree, that the deputies of color should take their seats in the assembly, or that England should have begun this great work, advantage might be taken of them, and the abolition of the Slave-trade might be resolved upon in the present session."

The last question I proposed was this. "If the

determination of this great question should be
proposed to the next legislature, would it be more
difficult to carry it then than now?"

This question also produced much conversation. But the answer was unanimous, "that there
would be no greater difficulty in the one than in
the other case; for that the people would daily,
more and more admire their constitution; that
this constitution would go down to the next legislature, from whence would issue solid and fixed
principles, which would be resorted to as a standard for decision on all occasions. Hence, the
Slave-trade, which would be adjudged by it also,
could not possibly stand. Add to which, that the
most virtuous members in the present would be
chosen into the new legislature, which, if the constitution were but once fairly established, would
not regard the murmurs of any town or province."
After this a desultory conversation took place, in
which some were of opinion that it would be
proper, on the introduction of the subject into
the assembly, to move for a committee of inquiry,
which should collect facts and documents against
the time, when it should be taken up with a view
to its final discussion.

As it now appeared to me that nothing material
would be done with respect to our cause till after
the election of the new legislature, I had thoughts
of returning to England to resume my journey in
quest of evidence; but I judged it right to communicate first with the Comte de Mirabeau and
the Marquis de la Fayette, both of whom would

have attended the meeting just mentioned, if unforeseen circumstances had not prevented them.

On conversing with the first, I found that he differed from those whom I had consulted. He thought that the question, on account of the nature and urgency of it, ought to be decided in the present legislature. This was so much his opinion, that he had made a determination to introduce it there himself; and had been preparing for his motion. He had already drawn up the outlines of a speech for the purpose; but was in want of circumstantial knowledge to complete it. With this knowledge he desired me to furnish him. He then put his speech into my hand; and wished me to take it home and peruse it. He wrote down also some questions, and he gave them to me directly afterwards, and begged I would answer them at my leisure.

On conversing with the latter, he said, that he believed with those at the meeting, that there would be no greater difficulty in carrying the question in the succeeding than in the present legislature. But this consideration afforded an argument for the immediate discussion of it: for it would make a considerable difference to suffering humanity, whether it were to be decided now or then. This was the moment to be taken to introduce it; nor did he think that they ought to be deterred from doing it, by any supposed clamors from some of the towns in France. The great body of the people admired the constitution; and would support any decisions, which were made in

strict conformity to its principles. With respect
to any committee of inquiry, he deprecated it.
The Slave-trade, he said, was not a trade. It dis-
honoured the name of commerce. It was piracy.
But if so, the question which it involved, was a
question of justice only; and it could not be decided with propriety by any other standard." I
then informed him, that the Comte de Mirabeau
had undertaken to introduce it into the assembly.
At this he expressed his uneasiness. "Mirabeau,"
says he, "is a host in himself; and I should not
be surprised if by his own eloquence and popu-
larity only, he were to carry it; and yet I regret
that he has taken the lead in it. The cause is so
lovely, that even ambition, abstractedly considered,
is too impure to take it under its protection, and
not to sully it. It should have been placed in
the hands of the most virtuous man in France.
This man is the Duke de la Rochefoucauld. But
you cannot alter things now. You cannot take it
out of his hands. I am sure he will be second to
no one on this occasion."

On my return to my hotel, I perused the outlines of the speech, which the Comte de Mirabeau
had lent me. It afforded a masterly knowledge
of the evils of the trade, as drawn from reason
only. It was put together in the most striking
and affecting manner. It contained an almost
irresistible appeal to his auditors by frequent refer-
ences to the ancient system of things in France,
and to their situation and prospects under the
new. It flowed at first gently like a river in a level

country; but it grew afterwards into a mountain torrent, and carried every thing before it. On looking at the questions, which he had written down for me, I found them consist of three. 1. What are the different ways of reducing to slavery the inhabitants of that part of Africa, which is under the dominion of France? 2. What is the state of society there with respect to government, industry, and the arts? 3. What are the various evils belonging to the transportation of the Africans from their own country?

It was peculiarly agreeable to me to find, on reading the first two questions, that I had formed an acquaintance with Monsieur Geoffroy de Villeneuve, who had been aide-du-camp to the Chevalier de Boufflers at Goree; but who was then at his father's house in Paris. This gentleman had entertained Dr. Spaarman and Mr. Wadstrom; and had accompanied them up the Senegal, when under the protection of the French government in Africa. He had confirmed to me the testimony, which they had given before the privy council. But he had a fund of information on this subject, which went far beyond what these possessed, or I had ever yet collected from books or men. He had travelled all over the kingdom of Cayor on foot; and had made a map of it. His information was so important, that I had been with him for almost days together to take it down. I determined therefore to arrange the facts which I had obtained from him, of which I had now a volume, that I might answer the two first questions which had been proposed to me; for it was of great importance to the Comte de Mirabeau, that he should be able to appeal in behalf of the statements in his speech to the assembly, to an evidence on the spot.

In the course of my correspondence with the comte, which continued with but little intermission for six weeks, many circumstances took place, which were connected with the cause, and which I shall now detail in their order.

On waiting upon M. Necker, at his own request, he gave me the pleasing intelligence, that the committee of finances, which was then composed of members of the National Assembly, had resolved, though they had not yet promulgated their resolution, upon a total abolition of all the bounties then in existence in favor of the Slave-trade.

The deputies of color now began to visit me at my own hotel. They informed me, that they had been admitted, since they had seen me, into the National Assembly. On stating their claims, the president assured them, that they might take courage; for that the assembly knew no distinction between blacks and whites, but considered all men as having equal rights. This speech of the president, they said, had roused all the white colonists in Paris. Some of these had openly insulted them. They had held also a meeting on the subject of this speech; at which they had worked themselves up so as to become quite furious. Nothing but intrigue was now going for-

ward among them to put off the consideration of
the claims of the free people of color. They, the
deputies, had been flattered by the prospect of a
hearing no less than six times; and, when the
day arrived, something had constantly occurred
to prevent it.

At a subsequent interview, they appeared to be
quite disheartened; and to be grievously disappointed as to the object of their mission. They
were now sure, that they should never be able to
make head against the intrigues and plots of the
white colonists. Day after day had been fixed as
before for the hearing of their cause. Day after
day it had been deferred in like manner. They
were now weary with waiting. One of them,
Ogé, could not contain himself, but broke out
with great warmth: "I begin," says he, "not
to care, whether the National Assembly will admit us or not. But let it beware of the consequences. We will no longer continue to be be-
held in a degraded light. Dispatches shall go
directly to St. Domingo; and we will soon follow
them. We can produce as good soldiers on our
estates, as those in France. Our own arms shall
make us independent and respectable. If we are
once forced to desperate measures, it will be in
vain that thousands will be sent across the Atlan-
tic to bring us back to our former state." On
hearing this, I entreated the deputies to wait with
patience. I observed to them, that in a great
revolution, like that of France, things, but more
particularly such as might be thought external.

could not be discussed either so soon or so rapidly
as men full of enthusiasm would wish. France
would first take care of herself. She would then,
I had no doubt, extend her care to her colonies.
Was not this a reasonable conclusion, when they,
the deputies, had almost all the first men in the
assembly in their favor? I entreated them therefore to wait patiently; as well as upon another
consideration, which was, that by an imprudent
conduct they might not only ruin their own cause
in France, but bring indescribable misery upon
their native land.

By this time a large packet, for which I had
sent from England, arrived. It consisted of above
a thousand of the plan and section of a slave-ship
with an explanation in French. It contained also
about five hundred colored engravings, made from
two views, which Mr. Wadstrom had taken in
Africa. The first of these represented the town
of Joal, and the king's military on horseback
returning to it, after having executed the great
pillage, with their slaves. The other represented
the village of Bain; from whence ruffians were
forcing a poor woman and her children to sell
them to a ship, which was then lying in the roads.
Both these scenes Mr. Wadstrom had witnessed.
I had collected also by this time, one thousand
of my Essays on the Impolicy of the Slave-trade,
which had been translated into the French language. These I now wished to distribute, as
preparatory to the motion of Mirabeau, among
the National Assembly. This distribution was

afterwards undertaken and effected by the arch-bishop of Aix, the bishop Chartres, the Marquis de la Fayette, the Duke de la Rochefoucauld, the Comte de Mirabeau, Monsieur Necker, the Marquis de Condorcet, Messieurs Petion de Villeneuve, Bergasse, Claviere and Brissot, and by the Mar-chioness de la Fayette, Madame Necker, and Mad-ame de Poivre, the latter of whom was the widow of the late Intendent of the Isle of France.

This distribution had not been long begun, be-fore I witnessed its effects. The virtuous Abbé Gregoire, and several members of the National Assembly, called upon me. The section of the slave-ship, it appeared, had been the means of drawing them towards me. They wished for more accurate information concerning it. Indeed it made its impression upon all who saw it. The bishop of Chartres once told me, that when he first espoused our cause, he did it at once; for it seemed obvious to him that no one could, under the Christian dispensation, hold another as his slave; and it was no less obvious, where such an unnatural state existed, that there would be great abuses; but that, nevertheless, he had not given credit to all the tales which had been related of the Slave-trade, till he had seen this plate; after which there was nothing so barbarous which might not readily be believed. The archbishop of Aix, when I first showed him the same plate, was so struck with horror, that he could scarcely speak: and when Mirabeau first saw it, he was so im-pressed by it, that he ordered a mechanic to make

a model of it in wood, at a considerable expense.
This model he kept afterwards in his dining room.
It was a ship in miniature, about a yard long, and
little wooden men and women, which were painted
black to represent the slaves, were seen stowed in
their proper places.

But while the distribution of these different
articles thus contributed to make us many friends,
it called forth the extraordinary exertions of our
enemies.   The merchants and others interested
in the continuance of the Slave-trade wrote letters
to the archbishop of Aix, beseeching him not to
ruin France; which he would inevitably do, if, as
then president, he were to grant a day for hearing the question of the abolition. Offers of money
were made to Mirabeau from the same quarter,
if he would totally abandon his motion.   An attempt was made to establish a colonial committee,
consisting of such planters as were members of
the National Assembly; upon whom it should
devolve to consider and report upon all matters
relating to the colonies, before they could be determined there.   Books were circulated in abun-
dance in opposition to mine.   Resort was again
had to the public papers, as the means of raising
a hue and cry against the principles of the Friends
of the Negroes. I was again denounced as a spy;
and as one sent by the English minister to bribe
members of the Assembly to do that in a time of
public agitation, which in the settled state of
France they could never have been prevailed upon
to accomplish.   And as a proof that this was my

errand, it was requested of every Frenchman to put to himself the following question, "How it happened that England, which had considered the subject coolly and deliberately for eighteen. months, and this in a state of internal peace and quietness, had not abolished the Slave-trade?"

The clamor which was now made against the abolition, pervaded all Paris, and reached the ears of the king. M. Necker had a long conversation with him upon it. The latter sent for me immediately. He informed me, that his majesty was desirous of making himself master of the question, and had expressed a wish to see my Essay on the Impolicy of the Slave-trade. He desired to have two copies of it; one in French and the other in English; and he would then take his choice as to which of them he would read. He (M. Necker) was to present them. He would take with him also at the same time the beautiful specimens of the manufactures of the Africans, which I had lent to Madame Necker out of the cabinet of Monsieur Geoffroy de Villeneuve and others. As to the section of the slave-ship, he thought it would affect his majesty too much, as he was then indisposed. All these articles, except the latter, were at length presented. The king bestowed a good deal of time upon the specimens. He admired them; but particularly those in gold. He expressed his surprise at the state of some of the arts in Africa. He sent them back on the same day on which he had examined them, and commissioned M. Necker to return me his

23*

thanks; and to say that he had been highly gratified with what he had seen; and, with respect to the Essay on the Impolicy of the Slave-trade, that he would read it with all the seriousness which such a subject deserved.

My correspondence with the Comte de Mirabeau was now drawing near to its close. I had sent him a letter every other day for a whole month, which contained from sixteen to twenty pages. He usually acknowledged the receipt of each. Hence many of his letters came into my possession. These were always interesting, on account of the richness of the expressions they contained. Mirabeau, even in his ordinary discourse, was eloquent. It was his peculiar talent to use such words, that they who heard them, were almost led to believe, that he had taken great pains to cull them for the occasion. But this his ordinary language was the language also of his letters; and as they show a power of expression, by which the reader may judge of the character of the eloquence of one, who was then undoubtedly the greatest orator in France, I have thought it not improper to submit one of them to his perusal in the annexed note.*   I could have

* "Je fais toujours mille remercimens plus empressés et plus affectueux à Monsieur Clarkson pour la vertueuse profusion de ses lumieres, de ses reserches, et de ses travaux. Comme ma motion et tous ses developpemens sont entierement prêts j'attends avec une vive impatience ses nouvelles lettres, afin d'achever de classer les faits et les raisonnemens de Monsieur Clarkson, et, cette deduction entierement finie, de commencer à manœuvrer en tactique le succès douteux de cette perilleuse proposition. J'aurai l'honneur

wished, as far as it relates to myself, that it had been less complimentary. It must be observed, however, that I had already written to him more than two hundred pages with my own hand; and as this was done at no small expense, time and trouble, and solely to qualify him for the office of doing good, he could not but set some value upon my labors.

When our correspondence was over, I had some conversation with him relative to fixing a day for the motion. But he judged it prudent, previously to this, to sound some of the members of the assembly on the subject of it. This he did; but he was greatly disappointed at the result. There was not one member, out of all those with whom he conversed, who had not been canvassed by the planter's committee. And though most of them had been proof against all its intrigues and artifices, yet many of them hesitated respecting the abolition at that moment. There was a fear in some that they should injure the revolution by adopting it; others, who had no such fears, wished for the concurrence of England in the measure, and suggested the propriety of a deputation there for that purpose previously to the discussion of the question in France. While others maintained, that as England had done nothing, after having

de le recevoir Dimanche depuis onze heures, et même dix du matin jusqu'à midi, non seulement avec un vif plaisir, mais avec une sensible reconnaissance.

"LE COMTE DE MIRABEAU.

"*Decembre* 25, 1789."

had it so long under consideration, it was fair to
presume, that she judged it impolitic to abandon
the Slave-trade; but if France were to give it up,
and England to continue it, how would humanity
be the gainer?

While the Comte de Mirabeau was continuing
his canvass among the members of the National
Assembly, relative to his motion, attempts were
again made in the public papers to mislead them.
Emancipation was now stated to be the object
of the Friends of the Negroes. This charge I re-
pelled, by addressing myself to Monsieur Beauvet.
I explained to him the views of the different societies, which had taken up the cause of the Africans; and I desired him to show my letter to the
planters. I was obliged also to answer publicly
a letter by Monsieur Mosneron de Laung. This
writer professed to detail the substance of the
privy council report. He had the injustice to assert, that three things had been distinctly proved
there: First, that slavery had always existed in
Africa; Secondly, that the natives were a bloody
people, addicted to human sacrifice, and other barbarous customs; and, thirdly, that their soil was
incapable of producing any proper articles for commerce. From these premises he argued, as if they
had been established by the unanimous and uncontradicted testimony of the witnesses; and he
drew the conclusion, that not only had England
done nothing in consequence, but that she never
would do any thing which should affect the existence of this trade.

But these letters had only just made their appearance in the public papers, when I was summoned to England. Parliament, it appeared, had met; and I was immediately to leave Paris. Among those, of whom I had but just time to take leave, were the deputies of color. At this, my last conference with them, I recommended moderation and forbearance, as the best gifts I could leave them; and I entreated them rather to give up their seats in the assembly, than on that account to bring misery on their country; for that with patience their cause would ultimately triumph. They replied, that I had prescribed to them a most difficult task. They were afraid that neither the conduct of the white colonists nor of the National Assembly could be much longer borne. They thanked me, however, for my advice. One of them gave me a trinket, by which I might remember him; and as for himself, he said, he should never forget one, who had taken such a deep interest in the welfare of his mother.* I found, however, notwithstanding all I said, that there was a spirit of dissatisfaction in them, which nothing but a redress of their grievances could subdue; and that, if the planters should persevere in their intrigues, and the National Assembly in delay, a fire would be lighted up in St. Domingo, which could not easily be extinguished. This was afterwards realized: for Ogé, in about three months from this time, left his companions to report to his constituents in St. Domingo the state

* Africa.

of their mission; when hearing, on his arrival in that island, of the outrageous conduct of the whites of the committee of Aquin, who had begun a persecution of the people of color, for no other reason than that they had dared to seek the common privileges of citizens; and of the murder of Ferrand and Labadie, he imprudently armed his slaves. With a small but faithful band he rushed upon superior numbers, and was defeated. Taking refuge at length in the Spanish part of St. Domingo, he was given up; and his enemies, to strike terror into the people of color, broke him upon the wheel. From this time reconciliation between the parties became impossible. A bloody war commenced, and with it all those horrors which it has been our lot so frequently to deplore. It must be remembered, however, that the Slave-trade, by means of the cruel distinctions it occasioned, was the original cause; and though the revolution of France afforded the occasion; it was an occasion which would have been prevented, if it had not been for the intrigues and injustice of the whites.

Another, upon whom I had time to call, was the amiable bishop of Chartres. When I left him, the Abbe Syeyes, who was with him, desired to walk with me to my hotel. He there presented me with a set of his works, which he sent for, while he staid with me; and on parting, he made use of this complimentary expression, in allusion, I suppose, to the cause I had undertaken: "I am

pleased to have been acquainted with the friend
of man."

It was necessary that I should see the Comte de
Mirabeau and the Marquis de la Fayette, before
I left Paris. I had written to each of them to
communicate the intelligence of my departure, as
soon as I received it. The comte, it appeared,
had nearly canvassed the assembly.. He could
count upon three hundred members, who, for the
sake of justice, and without any consideration of
policy or of consequences, would support his motion. But alas! what proportion did this number
bear to twelve hundred! About five hundred more
would support him; but only on one condition;
which was, if England would give an unequivocal
proof of her intention to abolish the trade. The
knowledge of these circumstances, he said, had induced him to write a letter to Mr. Pitt. In this
he had explained, how far he could proceed without his assistance, and how far with it. He had
frankly developed to him the mind and temper of
the assembly on this subject; but his answer must
be immediate; for the white colonists were daily
gaining such an influence there, that he foresaw it
would be impossible to carry the measure, if it were
long delayed. On taking leave of him he desired
me to be the bearer of the letter, and to present
it to Mr. Pitt.

On conversing with the Marquis de la Fayette,
he lamented deeply the unexpected turn which
the cause of the negroes had lately taken in the
assembly. It was entirely owing to the daily

intrigues of the white colonists. He feared they
would ruin every thing. If the deputies of color
had been heard on their arrival, their rights would
have been acknowledged. But now there was
little probability that they would obtain them. He
foresaw nothing but desolation in St. Domingo.
With respect to the abolition of the Slave-trade,
it might be yet carried; but not unless England
would concur in the measure. On this topic he
enlarged with much feeling. He hoped the day
was near at hand, when two great nations, which
had been hitherto distinguished only for their hostility, one toward the other, would unite in so sub
lime a measure; and that they would follow up
their union by another, still more lovely, for the
preservation of eternal and universal peace. Thus
their future rivalships might have the extraordinary merit of being rivalships in good. Thus the
revolution of France, through the mighty aid of
England, might become the source of civilization,
of freedom, and of happiness to the whole world.
No other nations were sufficiently enlightened for
such an union, but all other nations might be
benefited by it.

The last person whom I saw was Brissot. He
accompanied me to my carriage. With him therefore I shall end my French account; and I shall
end it in no way so satisfactory to myself, as in
a very concise vindication of his character, from
actual knowledge against the attacks of those who
have endeavored to disparage it; but who never
knew him. Justice and truth, I am convinced,

demand some little declaration on this subject
at my hands. Brissot then was a man of plain
and modest appearance. His habits, contrary to
those of his countrymen in general, were domestic.
In his own family he set an amiable example, both
as a husband and as a father. On all occasions he
was a faithful friend. He was particularly watch-
ful over his private conduct. From the simplicity
of his appearance, and the severity of his morals,
he was called The Quaker; at least in all the
circles which I frequented. He was a man of
deep feeling. He was charitable to the poor as
far as a slender income permitted him. But his
benevolence went beyond the usual bounds. He
was no patriot in the ordinary acceptation of the
word; for he took the habitable globe as his
country, and wished to consider every foreigner as
his brother.

I left France, as it may be easily imagined,
much disappointed, that my labors, which had
been of nearly six months' continuance, should
have had no better success; nor did I see in
looking forward, any circumstances that were
consoling with respect to the issue of them there;
for it was impossible that Mr. Pitt, even if he had
been inclined to write to Mirabeau, circumstanced
as matters then were with respect to the hearing
of evidence, could have given him a promise, at
least of a speedy abolition; and, unless his answer
had been immediate, it would have arrived, seeing
that the French planters were daily profiting by
their intrigues, too late to be effectual.

I had but just arrived in England, when Mr.
Wilberforce made a new motion in the House of
Commons on the subject of the Slave-trade. In
referring to the transactions of the last sessions,
he found that twenty-eight days had been allotted
to the hearing of witnesses against the abolition,
and that eleven persons only had been examined
in that time. If the examinations were to go on
in the same manner, they might be made to last
for years. He resolved therefore to move, that,
instead of hearing evidence in future in the house
at large, members should hear it in an open committee above stairs ; which committee should sit
notwithstanding any adjournment of the house itself. This motion he made ; and in doing it he
took an opportunity of correcting an erroneous
report ; which was, that he had changed his mind
on this great subject. This was, he said, so far
from being the case, that the more he contem-
plated the trade, the more enormous he found it,
and the more he felt himself compelled to persevere in endeavors for its abolition.

One would have thought that a motion, so reasonable and so constitutional, would have met
with the approbation of all; but it was vehe-
mently opposed by Mr. Gascoyne, alderman Newnham, and others. The plea set up was, that
there was no precedent for referring a question of
such importance to a committee. It was now
obvious, that the real object of our opponents in
abandoning decision by the privy council evidence
was delay. Unable to meet us there, they were

glad to fly to any measure, which should enable them to put off the evil day. This charge was fixed upon them in unequivocal language by Mr. Fox; who observed besides, that if the members of the house should then resolve to hear evidence in a committee of the whole house as before, it would amount to a resolution, that the question of the abolition of the Slave-trade should be put by, or at least that it should never be decided by them. After a long debate, the motion of Mr. Wilberforce was voted without a division; and the examination of witnesses proceeded in behalf of those who were interested in the continuance of the trade.

This measure having been resolved upon, by which dispatch in the examinations was promoted I was alarmed lest we should be called upon for our own evidence, before we were fully prepared. The time which I had originally allotted for the discovery of new witnesses, had been taken up, if not wasted, in France. In looking over the names of the sixteen, who were to have been examined by the committee of privy council if there had been time, one had died, and eight, who were sea-faring people, were out of the kingdom. It was time, therefore, to stir immediately in this business. Happily, on looking over my letters, which I found on my arrival in England, the names of several had been handed to me, with the places of their abode, who could give me information of the subject of our question. All these I visited with the utmost dispatch. I was absent only three weeks. I had travelled a thousand miles in this time, had conversed with seventeen persons, and had prevailed upon three to be examined.

I had scarcely returned with the addition of these witnesses to my list, when I found it necessary to go out again upon the same errand. This second journey arose in part from the following circumstances. There was a matter in dispute relative to the mode of obtaining slaves in the rivers of Calabar and Bonny. It was usual, when the slave-ships lay there, for a number of canoes to go into the inland country. These went in a fleet. There might be from thirty to forty armed natives in each of them. Every canoe also had a four or a six-pounder (cannon) fastened to her bow. Equipped in this manner they departed; and they were usually absent from eight to fourteen days. It was said that they went to fairs, which were held on the banks of these rivers, and at which there was a regular show of slaves. On their return they usually brought down from eight hundred to a thousand of these for the ships. These lay at the bottom of the canoes; their arms and legs having been first bound by the ropes of the country. Now the question was, how the people, thus going up these rivers, obtained their slaves?

It was certainly a very suspicious circumstance, that such a number of persons should go out upon these occasions; and that they should be armed in such a manner. We presumed therefore, that, though they might buy many of the slaves, whom they brought down, at the fairs, which have been mentioned, they obtained others by violence, as opportunity offered. This inference we pressed upon our opponents; and called upon them to show what circumstances made such warlike preparations necessary on these excursions. To this they replied readily. The people in the canoes, said they, pass through the territories of different petty princes; to each of whom, on entering his territory, they pay a tribute or toll. This tribute has been long fixed; but attempts frequently have been made to raise it. They who follow the trade cannot afford to submit to these unreasonable demands; and therefore they arm themselves in case of any determination on the part of these petty princes to enforce them.

This answer we never judged to be satisfactory. We tried, therefore, to throw light upon the subject, by inquiring if the natives, who went up on these expeditions, usually took with them as many goods as would amount to the number of the slaves they were accustomed to bring back with them. But we could get no direct answer, from any actual knowledge, to this question. All had seen the canoes go out and return; but no one had seen them loaded, nor had been on board them. It appeared, however, from circumstantial evidence, that though the natives on these occasions might take some articles of trade with them, it was impossible from appearances, that they could take them in the proportion mentioned.

24*

We maintained then our inference as before; but it was still uniformly denied.

How then were we to decide this important question? for it was said, that no white man was ever permitted by the natives to go up in these canoes. On mentioning accidentally the circumstances of the case, as I have now stated them, to a friend, immediately on my return from my last journey, he informed me, that he himself had been in company, about a year before, with a sailor, a very respectable looking man, who had been up these rivers. He had spent half an hour with him at an inn. He described his person to me. But he knew nothing of his name, or of the place of his abode. All he knew was, that he was either going, or that he belonged to, some ship of war in ordinary; but he could not tell at what port. I might depend upon all these circumstances, if the man had not deceived him; and he saw no reason why he should.

I felt myself set on fire, as it were, by this intelligence, deficient as it was; and I seemed to determine instantly that I would if it were possible, find him out. For if our suspicions were true, that the natives frequently were kidnapped in these expeditions, it would be of great importance to the cause of the abolition to have them confirmed; for as many slaves came annually from these two rivers, as from all the coast of Africa besides. But how to proceed on so blind an errand was the question. I first thought of trying to trace the man by letter. But this might be tedious. The examinations were now going on rapidly. We should soon be called upon for evidence ourselves. Besides, I knew nothing of his name. I then thought it to be a more effectual way to apply to Sir Charles Middleton, as comptroller of the navy, by whose permission I could board every ship of war in ordinary in England, and judge for myself. But here the undertaking seemed very arduous; and the time it would consume became an objection in this respect, that I thought I could not easily forgive myself, if I were to fail in it. My inclination, however, preponderated this way. At length I determined to follow it; for, on deliberate consideration, I found that I could not employ my time more advantageously to the cause; for as other witnesses must be found out somewhere, it was highly probable that, if I should fail in the discovery of this man, I should, by moving among such a number of seafaring people, find others, who could give their testimony in our favor.

I must now inform the reader, that ships of war in ordinary, in one of which this man was reported to be, are those, which are out of commission, and which are laid up in the different rivers and waters in the neighborhood of the king's dockyards. Every one of these have a boatswain, gunner, carpenter, and assistants on board. They lie usually in divisions of ten or twelve; and a master in the navy has a command over every division.

At length I began my journey. I boarded all

the ships of war lying in ordinary at Deptford, and examined the different persons in each. From Deptford I proceeded to Woolwich, where I did the same. Thence I hastened to Chatham, and then, down the Medway, to Sheerness. I had now boarded above a hundred and sixty vessels of war. I had found out two good and willing evidences among them. But I could gain no intelligence of him who was the object of my search.

From Chatham, I made the best of my way to Portsmouth harbor. A very formidable task presented itself here. But the masters' boats were ready for me ; and I continued my pursuit. On boarding the Pegase, on the second day, I discovered a very respectable person in the gunner of that ship. His name was George Millar. He had been on board the Canterbury slave-ship at the dreadful massacre at Calabar. He was the only disinterested evidence living, of whom I had yet heard. He expressed his willingness to give his testimony, if his presence should be thought necessary in London. I then continued my pursuit for the remainder of the day. On the next day, I resumed and finished it for this quarter. I had now examined the different persons in more than a hundred vessels in this harbor, but I had not discovered the person I had gone to seek.

Matters now began to look rather disheartening, I mean, as far as my grand object was concerned. There was but one other port left, and this was between two and three hundred miles distant. I determined, however, to go to Plymouth. I had already been more successful in this tour, with respect to obtaining general evidence, than in any other of the same length; and the probability was, that, as I should continue to move among the same kind of people, my success would be in a similar proportion according to the number visited. These were great encouragements to me to proceed. At length I arrived at the place of my last hope. On my first day's expedition I boarded forty vessels, but found no one in these who had been on the coast of Africa in the Slave-trade. One or two had been there in king's ships; but they had never been on shore. Things were now drawing near to a close; and notwithstanding my success as to general evidence in this journey, my heart began to beat. I was restless and uneasy during the night. The next morning, I felt agitated again between the alternate pressure of hope and fear; and in this state I entered my boat. The fifty-seventh vessel, which I boarded in this harbor, was the Melampus frigate. One person belonging to it, on examining him in the captain's cabin, said he had been two voyages to Africa; and I had not long discoursed with him, before I found, to my inexpressible joy, that he was the man. I found too, that he unravelled the question in dispute precisely as our inferences had determined it. He had been two expeditions up the river Calabar in the canoes of the natives. In the first of these, they came within a certain distance of a village. They then concealed them-

selves under the bushes, which hung over the
water from the banks. In this position they remained during daylight. But at night they went
up to it armed, and seized all the inhabitants, who
had not time to make their escape. They obtained
forty-five persons in this manner. In the second,
they were out eight or nine days; when they
made a similar attempt, and with nearly similar
success. They seized men, women, and children,
as they could find them in the huts. They then
bound their arms, and drove them before them to
the canoes. The name of the person, thus discovered on board the Melampus, was Isaac Parker.
On inquiring into his character from the master
of the division, I found it highly respectable. I
found also, afterwards, that he had sailed with
Captain Cook, with great credit to himself, round
the world. It was also remarkable that my
brother, on seeing him in London, when he went
to deliver his evidence, recognised him as having
served on board the Mornach man-of-war, and as
one of the most exemplary men in that ship.

I returned now in triumph. I had been out
only three weeks, and I had found out this extraordinary person, and five respectable witnesses
besides. These, added to the three discovered in
the last journey, and to those provided before,
made us more formidable than at any former period; so that the delay of our opponents, which
we had looked upon as so great an evil, proved in
the end truly serviceable to our cause.

On going into the committee room of the House

of Commons on my return, I found that the examinations were still going on in the behalf of those who were interested in the continuance of the trade; and they went on beyond the middle of April, when it was considered that they had closed. Mr. Wilberforce moved accordingly on the twenty-third of the same month, that Captain Thomas Wilson, of the royal navy, and that Charles Berns Wadstrom and Henry Hew Dalrymple, esquires, do attend as witnesses on the behalf of the abolition. There was nothing now but clamor from those on the opposite side of the question. They knew well, that there were but few members of the House of Commons, who had read the privy council report. They knew therefore, that, if the question were to be decided by evidence, it must be decided by that, which their own witnesses had given before Parliament. But this was the evidence only on one side. It was certain, therefore, if the decision were to be made upon this basis, that it must be entirely in their favor. Will it then be believed that in an English House of Commons there could be found persons, who could move to prevent the hearing of any other witnesses on this subject; and, what is more remarkable, that they should charge Mr. Wilberforce, because he proposed the hearing of them, with the intention solely of delay? Yes. Such persons were found, but, happily, only among the friends of the Slave-trade. Mr. Wilberforce, in replying to them, could not help observing, that it was rather extraordinary that they, who had

occasioned the delay of a whole year, should'
charge him with that of which they themselves·
had been so conspicuously guilty. He then commented for some time on the injustice of their
motion. He stated, too, that he would undertake
to remove from disinterested and unprejudiced
persons many of the impressions which had been
made by the witnesses against the abolition; and
he appealed to the justice and honor of the house
in behalf of an injured people; under the hope,
that they would not allow a decision to be made
till they had heard the whole of the case. These
observations, however, did not satisfy all those
who belonged to the opposite party. Lord Penrhyn
contended for a decision without a moment's delay. Mr. Gascoyne relented, and said he would
allow three weeks to abolitionists, during which
their evidence might be heard. At length the
debate ended; in the course of which, Mr. Pitt
and Mr. Fox powerfully supported Mr. Wilber-·
force; when the motion was negatived without
any attempt at a division.

The witnesses in behalf of the abolition of the
Slave-trade now took possession of the ground,
which those in favor of it had left. But what
was our surprise, when only three of them had
been heard, to find that Mr. Norris should come
forward as an evidence! This he did to confirm
what he had stated to the privy council as to the
general question; but he did it more particularly,
as it appeared afterward, in the justification of his
own conduct: for the part which he had taken

at Liverpool, as it related to me, had become a
subject of conversation with many. It was now
well known what assistance he had given me
there in my pursuit; how he had even furnished
me with clauses for a bill for the abolition of the
trade; how I had written to him, in consequence
of his friendly co-operation, to come up as an evidence in our favor; and how at that moment he
had accepted the office of a delegate on the contrary side. The noise, which the relation and
repetition of these and other circumstances had
made, had given him, I believe, considerable pain.
His friends, too, had urged some explanation as
necessary. But how short-sighted are they who do
wrong! By coming forward in this imprudent
manner, he fixed the stain only the more indelibly
on himself; for he thus imposed upon me the
cruel necessity of being examined against him;
and this necessity was the more afflicting to me,
because I was to be called upon, not to state facts
relative to the trade, but to destroy his character
as an evidence in its support. I was to be called
upon, in fact, to explain all those communications,
which have been stated to have taken place between us on this subject. Glad, indeed, should I
have been to have declined this painful interference. But no one would hear of a refusal. The
bishop of London, Mr. Pitt, and Mr. Wilberforce,
considered my appearance on this occasion as an
imperious duty to the cause of the oppressed.
It may be perhaps sufficient to say, that I was
examined; that Mr. Norris was present all the

time; that I was cross-examined by counsel; and
that after this time, Mr. Norris seemed to have no
ordinary sense of his own degradation; for he
never afterwards held up his head, or looked the
abolitionists in the face, or acted with energy as
a delegate, as on former occasions.

The hearing of evidence continued to go on in
behalf of the abolition of the trade. No less than
twenty-four witnesses, altogether, were heard in
this session. And here it may not be improper
to remark, that during the examination of our
own witnesses as well as the cross-examination
of those of our opponents, no council were ever
employed. Mr. Wilberforce and Mr. William
Smith undertook this laborious department; and
as they performed it with great ability, so they
did it with great liberality towards those who
were obliged to come under their notice in the
course of this fiery ordeal.

The bill of Sir William Dolben was now to be
renewed. On this occasion the enemies of the
abolition became again conspicuous; for on the
twenty-sixth of May, they availed themselves of
a thin house to propose an amendment, by which
they increased the number of the slaves to the
tonnage of the vessel. They increased it too,
without taking into the account, as had hitherto
been done, the extent of the superficies of the
vessels which were to carry them. This was the
third indecorous attempt against what were only
reasonable and expected proceedings in the present
session. But their advantage was of no great

duration; for, the very next day, the amendment was rejected on the report by a majority of ninety-five to sixty-nine, in consequence, principally of the private exertions of Mr. Pitt.   Of this bill, though it was renewed in other years besides the present, I shall say no more in this history; because it has nothing to do with the general question.   Horrible as it yet left the situation of the poor slaves in their transportation, (which the plate has most abundantly shown,) it was the best bill which could be then obtained; and it answered to a certain degree the benevolent wishes of the worthy baronet who introduced it: for if we could conclude that these voyages were made more comfortable to the injured Africans, in proportion as there was less mortality in them, he had undoubtedly the pleasure of seeing the end, at least, partially, obtained; though he must always have felt a great drawback from it, by reflecting that the survivors, however their sufferings might have been a little diminished, were reserved for slavery.

The session was now near its close; and we had the sorrow to find, though we had defeated our opponents in the three instances which have been mentioned, that the tide ran decidedly against us, upon the general question, in the House of Commons.   The same statements, which had struck so many members with panic in the former sessions, such as that of emancipation, of the ruin and massacre of the planters, and of indemnification to the amount of seventy millions, had been industriously kept up, and this by a personal canvass among them. But this hostile disposition was still unfortunately increased by considerations of another sort. For the witnesses of our opponents had taken their ground first. No less than eleven of them had been examined in the last sessions. In the present, two-thirds of the time had been occupied by others on the same side. Hence the impression upon this ground also was against us; and we had yet had no adequate opportunity of doing it away. A clamor was also raised, where we thought it least likely to have originated. They (the planters) it was said, had produced persons in elevated life, and of the highest character as witnesses; whereas we had been obliged to take up with those of the lowest condition. This idea was circulated directly after the introduction of Isaac Parker, before mentioned; a simple mariner; and who was now contrasted with the admirals on the other side of the question. This outcry was not only ungenerous, but unconstitutional. It is the glory of the English law, that it has no scale of veracity, which it adapts to persons, according to the station, which they may be found to occupy in life. In our courts of law the poor are heard as well as the rich; and if their reputation be fair, and they stand proof against the cross-examinations they undergo, both the judge and the jury must determine the matter in dispute by their evidence. But the House of Commons were now called upon by our opponents, to adopt the preposterous maxim of attaching falsehood to poverty, or of weighing truth by the standard of rank and riches.

But though we felt a considerable degree of pain in finding this adverse disposition among so many members of the lower house, it was some consolation to us to know that our cause had not suffered with their constituents, the people. These were still warmly with us. Indeed, their hatred of the trade had greatly increased. Many circumstances had occurred in this year to promote it. The committee during my absence in France, had circulated the plate of the slave-ship throughout all England. No one saw it but he was impressed. It spoke to him in a language, which was at once intelligible and irresistible. It brought forth the tear of sympathy in behalf of the sufferers, and it fixed their sufferings in his heart. The committee, too, had been particularly vigilant during the whole of the year, with respect to the public papers. They had suffered no statement in behalf of those interested in the continuance of the trade, to go unanswered. Dr. Dickson, the author of the Letters on Slavery before mentioned, had come forward again with his services on this occasion, and by his active co-operation with a sub-committee appointed for the purpose, the coast was so well cleared of our opponents, that though they were seen the next year again, through the medium of the same papers, they appeared only in sudden incursions, as it were, during which they darted a few weapons at us; but they never afterwards ventured upon the plain to dispute the

matter, inch by inch, or point by point, in an open
and manly manner.

But other circumstances occurred to keep up a
hatred of the trade among the people in this interval, which, trivial as they were, ought not to
be forgotten. The amiable poet, Cowper, had
frequently made the Slave-trade the subject of
his contemplation. He had already severely condemned it in his valuable poem, The Task. But
now he had written three little fugitive pieces
upon it. Of these the most impressive was that
which he called The Negro's Complaint, and of
which the following is a copy :

> "Forc'd from home and all its pleasures,
>   Affic's coast I left forlorn,
> To increase a stranger's treasures,
>   O'er the raging billows borne;
>   Men from England bought and sold me,
>   Paid my price in paltry gold;
>   But, though theirs they have enroll'd me,
>   Minds are never to be sold.
>
> "Still in thought as free as ever,
>   What are England's rights, I ask,
> Me from my delights to sever,
>   Me to torture, me to task?
> Fleecy locks and black complexion
>   Cannot forfeit nature's claim;
> Skins may differ, but affection
>   Dwells in black and white the same.
>
> "Why did all-creating nature
>   Make the plant, for which we toil?
> Sighs must fan it, tears must water,
>   Sweat of ours must dress the soil.

Think, ye masters, iron-hearted,
   Lolling at your jovial boards,
Think, how many backs have smarted
   For the sweets your cane affords.

"Is there, as you sometimes tell us,
   Is there one, who rules on high;
Has he bid you buy and sell us,
   Speaking from his throne, the sky?
Ask him, if your knotted scourges,
   Fetters, blood-extorting screws,
Are the means, which duty urges
   Agents of his will to use?

"Hark! he answers. Wild tornadoes,
   Strewing yonder sea with wrecks,
Wasting towns, plantations, meadows,
   Are the voice with which he speaks.
He, foreseeing what vexations
   Afric's sons should undergo,
Fix'd their tyrant's habitations
   Where his whirlwinds answer—No.

"By our blood in Afric wasted,
   Ere our necks receiv'd the chain;
By the miseries, which we tasted
   Crossing, in your barks, the main;
By our sufferings, since you brought us
   To the man-degrading mart,
All sustain'd by patience, taught us
   Only by a broken heart:

"Deem our nation brutes no longer,
   Till some reason you shall find
Worthier of regard, and stronger,
   Than the color of our kind.
Slaves of gold! whose sordid dealings
   Tarnish all your boasted powers,
Prove that you have human feelings,
   Ere you proudly question ours."

This little piece Cowper presented in manuscript to some of his friends in London; and
these, conceiving it to contain a powerful appeal
in behalf of the injured Africans, joined in printing
it. Having ordered it on the finest hot-pressed
paper, and folded it up in a small and neat form,
they gave it the printed title of "A Subject for
Conversation at the Tea-table." After this, they
sent many thousand copies of it in franks into
the country. From one it spread to another, till
it travelled almost over the whole island. Falling
at length into the hands of the musician, it was
set to music; and it then found its way into the
streets, both of the metropolis and of the country,
where it was sung as a ballad; and where it gave
a plain account of the subject, with an appropriate feeling, to those who heard it.

Nor was the philanthropy of the late Mr. Wedgwood less instrumental in turning the popular
feeling in our favor. He made his own manufac-
tory contribute to this end. He took the seal of
the committee, as exhibited in this volume, for his
model; and he produced a beautiful cameo, of a
less size, of which the ground was a most delicate
white, but the negro, who was seen imploring
compassion in the middle of it, was in his own
native color. Mr. Wedgwood made a liberal do-
nation of these, when finished, among his friends.
I received from him no less than five hundred of
them myself. They, to whom they were sent,
did not lay them up in their cabinets, but gave
them away likewise. They were soon, like The

Negro's Complaint, in different parts of the kingdom. Some had them inlaid in gold on the lid
of their snuff-boxes. Of the ladies several wore
them in bracelets, and others had them fitted up
in an ornamental manner as pins for the hair.
At length, the taste for wearing them became
general; and thus fashion, which usually confines
itself to worthless things, was seen for once in
the honorable office of promoting the cause of
justice, humanity, and freedom.

I shall now only state that the committee took
as members within its own body, in the period
of time which is included in this chapter, the
reverend Mr. Ormerod, chaplain to the bishop of
London, and Captain James Bowen, of the royal
navy; that they elected the honorable Nathaniel
Curzon (now Lord Scarsdale), Dr. Frossard of
Lyons, and Benjamin Garlike, esquire, then secretary to the English embassy at the Hague, honorary and corresponding members; and that they
concluded their annual labors with a suitable
report; in which they noticed the extraordinary
efforts of our opponents to injure our cause, in the
following manner: "In the progress of this business a powerful combination of interest has been
excited against us. The African trader, the
planter, and the West India merchant have united
their forces to defend the fortress, in which their
supposed treasures lie. Vague calculations and
false alarms have been thrown out to the public,
in order to show that the constitution and even
the existence of this free and opulent nation de-

pend on its depriving the inhabitants of a foreign country of those rights, and of that liberty, which we ourselves so highly and so justly prize. Surely in the nature of things and in the order of Providence it cannot be so. England existed as a great nation, long before the African commerce was known amongst us, and it is not to acts of injustice and violence that she owes her present rank in the scale of nations."

END OF VOL. II.

BOOKS

PUBLISHED AND FOR SALE BY

JOHN S. TAYLOR,

THEOLOGICAL AND SUNDAY SCHOOL BOOKSELLER,

BRICK CHURCH CHAPEL,

CORNER OF PARK-ROW AND NASSAU-STREET,

OPPOSITE THE CITY HALL, NEW-YORK.

Hints to Parents on the Early Religious Education of Children. By GARDINER SPRING, D. D., Pastor of the Brick Presbyterian Church, New-York. 18mo. with a steel engraving. Price 37½ cts.

From the New-York Weekly Messenger and Young Men's Advocate.

Dr. Spring's Hints to Parents.—One of the prettiest little works of this class that we have ever met with, is just published; it is called "*Hints to Parents on the Religious Education of Children.* By Gardiner Spring, D. D." The author has been long and favorably known to the public as a chaste, powerful, and popular writer. The subject of the present work is one of great moment—one in which every parent has a real interest. And we commend this little volume, not only to pious parents, but to all who desire to bring up their children in such a manner as to make them an honor to themselves and a blessing to their fellow-men.

3

From the Commercial Advertiser.

Hints to Parents, on the Religious Education of Children. By Gardiner Spring, D. D. This beautiful little volume, coming out at this time, will be peculiarly acceptable to the congregation of the able and excellent author, and will have the effect of a legacy of his opinions on a most important subject, now that for a time they are deprived of his personal instructions. It is a work that should be in the hands of every parent throughout our country, who has the temporal and eternal interest of his offspring at heart. The few and leading maxims of the Christian religion are plainly and practically enforced, and the parent's duties are descanted on in a train of pure and beautiful eloquence, which a father's mind, elevated by religion, only could have dictated. We believe that a general knowledge of this little volume would be attended with consequences beneficial to society, since a practice of its recommendations could scarcely be refused to its solemn and affectionate spirit of entreaty.

The Ministry we Need. By S. H. Cox, D. D., and others. 37½ cents.

From the Literary and Theological Review.

This neat little volume comprises the inaugural charge and address which were delivered on occasion of inducting the PROFESSOR OF SACRED RHETORIC AND PASTORAL THEOLOGY in the Theological Seminary at Auburn. The friends of Dr. Cox will not be disappointed in his inaugural address. It bears the impress of his talents and piety—his enlarged views and catholic spirit. To analyze it would convey no adequate idea of its merits. His theme is the ministry of reconciliation—"the chosen medium by which God conciliates men—the mighty moral enginery that accomplishes his brightest wonders—the authentic diplomacy of the *King of kings* working salvation in the midst of the earth." The manner in which he treats his subject, in relation to the importance of the Christian ministry, and the kind of ministry needed in this age and nation, we need hardly remark will amply repay the perusal of his brethren, if not be interesting and instructive to the church at large.

"Error scenting notoriety" may not altogether like the

odor of this little book; and the "*lynx-eyed detecters of heresy*" will not be forward to approve a work in which they are handled with unsparing severity; but by "all the favorers on principle of a pious, sound, educated, scriptural, and accomplished ministry in the church of God, and throughout the whole world, as the MINISTRY WE NEED, to whom this little volume is most respectfully inscribed," it will be read, and, we trust, circulated.

The Christian's Pocket Companion.—

Selected from the works of JOHN ROGERS, Dr. OWEN, DAVID BRAINERD, PRESIDENT EDWARDS, and others, with an Introduction by Rev. JOHN BLATCHFORD, of Bridgeport, Conn. 25 cents.

The following is from Mr. Blatchford's Letter to the Publisher:

I am happy to learn, through your letter of last evening, your design of publishing the little work containing the private rules by which the lives of such men as Edwards, and Brainerd, and Rogers, and Mason, were regulated.

That little volume (which is the only copy that I have ever met with) was, for many of the last years of his life, the pocket-companion of my honored father, the late Samuel Blatchford, D. D. of Lansingburgh. This circumstance alone would give it a value in my estimation—as also with the many who were associated with him as a father in the ministry, as well as those who were permitted to receive "the message of salvation from his lips."

But in addition to this, who is there that loves the cause of Christ and the souls of men among the ministers of the Lord Jesus in our day, that has not often, amid the toils and discouragements and anxieties which so thickly beset their path, turned away to such men, and inquired the secret, if any there was, by which they accomplished so much for the Church, and secured to themselves a character for such eminent holiness? This little book answers these questions, and introduces us to these "men of God," in the closet, in the family, in the social circle, in the labors of the pulpit, and in the discharge of their multiplied parochial duties; and I am confident that no one can rise from its perusal without being incited to more prayer and more diligence in their varied efforts to adorn the "doctrines of Christ their Savior" themselves, and in preaching Christ and him crucified to others.

Wishing you all success in your undertaking, I would most fervently commend it to the blessing of God, believing that in giving it to the public, you will greatly subserve the best of causes, and in a very acceptable manner.

JOHN BLATCHFORD.

From the New-York Observer.

Christian's Pocket-Companion.—This very small but neat manual, just published, is a compilation of some of the purest sentiments and holiest aspirations of such men as Owen, Rogers, Brainerd, and President Edwards. We venture to say that no Christian can make it the familiar companion of his *heart*, as well as "pocket," without becoming evidently a holier and a happier man.

Practical Thoughts. By the late Dr. Nevins, of Baltimore. 50 cents.

Thoughts on Popery. By Dr. Nevins. 50 cts.

From the New-York Observer of April 9th, 1836.

The *Practical Thoughts* consists of forty-six articles on prayer, praise, professing Christ, duties to Sabbath Schools, the monthly concert, the conversion of the world, violations of the Sabbath, liberality, man's inconsistency, the pity of the Lord, Christian duty, death, &c.; the last of which are "Heaven's Attractions" and "The Heavenly Recognition," closing with the words, "By the time we have done what I recommend, we shall be close upon the celestial confines—perhaps within heaven's limits." * * *

There the sainted author laid down his pen, leaving the article unfinished, and went, none can doubt, to enjoy the blessed reality of the scenes he had been so vividly describing.

These articles combine great simplicity, attractiveness, and vivacity of thought and style, with a spiritual unction scarcely to be found in any other writer. Thousands of minds were impressed with them as they first appeared: they reproved the inconsistent Christian, roused the slumbering, and poured a precious balm into many an afflicted bosom. While writing them, the author buried a beloved wife, and had daily more and more sure indications that the hour of his own departure was at hand; and God enabled him, from the depths of his own Christian experience, to open rich fountains of blessing for others.

The *Thoughts on Popery* are like, and yet unlike, the other series. There is the same sprightliness of the imagination, the same clearness, originality, and richness of thought, with a keenness of argument, and sometimes irony, that exposes the baseness and shamelessness of the dogmas and superstitions of Popery, and that must carry home conviction to the understanding and heart of every unprejudiced reader. Piece by piece the delusion, not to say imposition, of that misnamed church are exposed, under the heads of the Sufficiency of the Bible, the Nine Commandments, Mortal and Venial Sins, Infallibility, Idolatry, Relics, the Seven Sacraments, Penance, the Mass, Celibacy of the Clergy, Purgatory, Canonizing Saints, Lafayette not at Rest, The Leopold Reports, Supererogation, Convents, &c. We know of nothing that has yet been issued which so lays open the deformities of Popery to common minds, or is so admirably adapted to save our country from its wiles, and to guard the souls of men from its fatal snares.

A View of the American Slavery Question. By E. P. Barrows, Pastor of the First Free Presbyterian Church. 31¼ cents.

From the New-York American of March 26th, 1836.

A View of the American Slavery Question, by E. P. BARROWS, Jun. Pastor of the First Free Presbyterian Church, New-York.—JOHN S. TAYLOR. In this little volume is embodied the substance of two discourses, preached, as we learn from the Introduction, "by the Author, in October, 1835, with particular reference to the condition of his own church." "Their result was a spirit of harmony and good feeling in the church." Such will not, we apprehend, be the result of their publication; for they maintain modestly, but firmly and conscientiously, the right and duty of reasoning and remonstrating with our

southern brethren against the enormity of slavery, and of
urging, in all lawful ways, its extinction. The North—
partly from mercenary and partly from political motives,
and with too many, perhaps, from culpable indifference—
seem anxious to stultify all their past efforts against slavery, and yield up even the right of discussing its evils,
and exhorting to its abandonment; and hence Mr. Barrows' modest and sincere efforts will not be very welcome
to northern recusants, while its doctrines will of course be
abhorrent to that chivalrous region where slavery is deemed
an ornament and a privilege. Nevertheless, Mr. Barrows
may console himself with having borne his testimony to
the truth.

Pleasure and Profit, vol. 1, or THE MUSEUM.
By Uncle Arthur. 37½ cents.

Pleasure and Profit, vol. 2, or THE BOY'S
FRIEND. By Uncle Arthur. 37½ cents.

Pleasure and Profit, vol. 3, or MARY AND
FLORENCE. By Uncle Arthur. 37½ cents.

Missionary Remains, or SKETCHES OF EVARTS,
CORNELIUS, AND WISNER. By Gardiner Spring, D. D.
and others. 37½ cents.

Advice to a Brother. By a Missionary. Price
31 cents.

Early Piety. By Rev. Jacob Abbott. 18¾ cents.

Scripture Gems. Morocco, gilt. 25 cents.

Sermons by Rev. Charles G. Finney. With a
Portrait. $1 00.

The Works of Rev. Daniel A. Clark.
In three volumes. $3 00.

Prevailing Prayer. By Rev. C. G. Finney. 32mo. 25 cents.

The National Preacher, printed in an elegant pamphlet form, each number containing two Sermons from living Ministers. Monthly. Edited by Rev. Austin Dickinson. Price one dollar a year in advance.

Also Publisher of

The **Cabinet of Freedom.** Under the supervision of the Hon. WILLIAM JAY, Rev. Prof. BUSH, of the University of New-York, and GERRIT SMITH, Esq. Terms, two dollars per annum, payable in advance.

Also Agent for

The Sabbath School Visiter, published by the Massachusetts Sabbath School Society. Edited by Rev. Asa Bullard, Boston. 50 cents.

Also Agent for

The Missionary Herald. Published for the American Board of Commissioners for Foreign Missions. Monthly. $1 50 a year.

Also Publisher of

The Naval Magazine. Edited by the Rev. C. S. Stewart, M. A. of the U. S. Navy. $3 00 a year, payable in advance.

J. S. T. has also a large and choice selection of Miscellaneous works, suitable for Sunday School Libraries; together with Theological, Classical, Moral, and Religious Books, Stationary, &c. all of which he will sell at the lowest prices.

A constant supply of the Publications of the Massachusetts Sabbath School Society, the American Sunday School

Union, and of the Protestant Episcopal Sunday School Union, at the same prices as sold at their respective Depositories.

N. B. Orders from the country will be immediately attended to, and books forwarded according to directions. Should the selection of books for Sunday Schools be left with J. S. T., and he should forward any which should not suit the purchaser, they may be returned, and the money will be refunded, or other books given in exchange. Those wishing to purchase, are invited to call and examine his stock.

Lightning Source UK Ltd.
Milton Keynes UK
UKHW022308080223
416651UK00001B/279